NORWEGIAN-AMERICAN STUDIES

The Journal of the Norwegian American Historical Association

2024

Since 1926, the Norwegian American Historical Association's journal *Norwegian-American Studies* has detailed and interpreted the Norwegian-American experience. It remains focused on showcasing new scholarship in the field of Norwegian-American studies, including the related fields of history, literature, religion, art, and cultural studies. The journal aims to not only publish scholarship on Norwegian-American life, but also facilitate intellectual exchange by publishing original research articles alongside discussions of scholarly works in progress, the teaching and learning of Norwegian-American studies, reviews of books recently published in the field, and more.

Norwegian-American Studies (ISSN 0078–1983) is published annually in the fall (Northern Hemisphere) by the University of Minnesota Press and is a benefit of membership in the Norwegian American Historical Association. For current subscription rates please see our website at https://www.upress.umn.edu. Digital subscriptions are available online through the Project MUSE Hosted Journals Program at https://muse.jhu.edu/.

If ordering by mail, please make checks payable to the University of Minnesota Press and send to

Norwegian-American Studies
University of Minnesota Press
111 Third Avenue South, Suite 290
Minneapolis, MN 55401–2520

Address subscription orders, changes of address, and business correspondence (including requests for permission and advertising orders) to the University of Minnesota Press, attention *Norwegian-American Studies*.

Author guidelines and submission preparation materials can be found on the Norwegian American Historical Association website at https://naha.stolaf.edu/pubs/guidelines.htm. Direct submissions to the journal editor at naha-editor@stolaf.edu.

NAHA Norwegian American Historical Association

The Norwegian American Historical Association (NAHA) is internationally recognized for its major role in furthering the academic study of Norwegian Americans. Since its founding in 1925, NAHA has been dedicated to collecting, preserving, and interpreting the Norwegian-American experience. The NAHA Archives are the largest designated repository for materials about Norwegian-American history and culture in North America. The Association also boasts a robust publications program, including the publication of notable book manuscripts, the academic journal *Norwegian-American Studies,* and a quarterly newsletter. NAHA's work is supported by an active and thriving membership. NAHA is located in the Rolvaag Library on the St. Olaf College campus in Northfield, MN. To learn more, please visit its website at https://naha.stolaf.edu.

CONTENTS

Norwegian-American Studies 42 • 2024

PHOTOGRAPH FEATURE

The Trane Story: Immigrant Entrepreneur to Global Giant

Ann Marie Legreid

James Trane (1857–1936) emigrated with his parents and siblings from Målselv Parish, Troms, Norway in 1864, ultimately settling on a small farm in western Wisconsin near the bustling river city of La Crosse.[1] Anxious to make his own way in the world, Trane left the farm to find employment in La Crosse, first apprenticing with the W. A. Roosevelt Company, where he worked as a plumber and steam pipefitter, and subsequently working in the city as a journeyman. With new skills in plumbing engineering, he opened his own plumbing firm in 1886 on Pearl Street in downtown La Crosse, not far from the Mississippi docks. The city's strong commercial base, coupled with a steady stream of immigrant workers, provided an excellent business site for Trane.

Norwegians in the city composed a large share of Trane's employees and clientele, but those profiles also included sizable numbers of Germans, the Dutch, other Europeans, and Old Americans. Trane advertised aggressively in

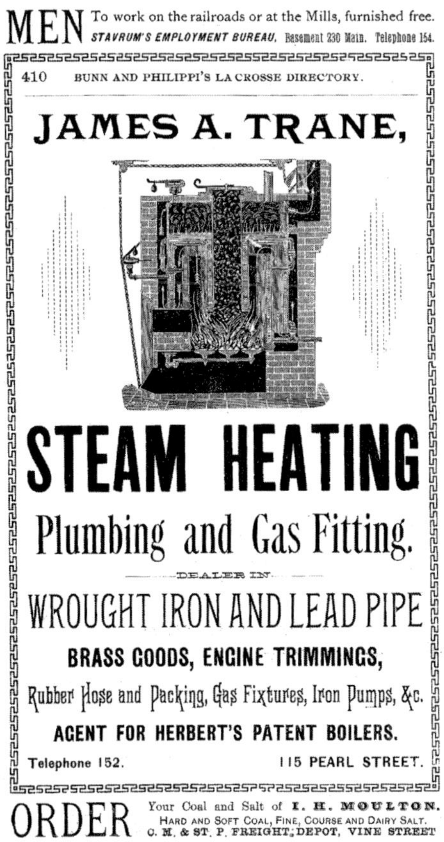

Figure 1. Trane advertisement in the 1888 La Crosse City Directory, page 410. James A. Trane Steam Heating, Plumbing, and Gas Fitting. Courtesy of the La Crosse Public Library Archives.

Figure 2. James Trane, founding father, built his company by taking giant strides in product innovation. His hard work, mechanical know-how, and entrepreneurial spirit were central to his success. Between James and his son, Reuben, the Tranes filed nearly thirty U.S. patents in heating and cooling technologies. Courtesy of the La Crosse Public Library Archives.

Figure 3. Jas. A. Trane Plumbing-Steam & Hot Water Heating opened for business on 118 Pearl Street, La Crosse, in 1886. Courtesy of the La Crosse Public Library Archives.

the local newspaper, the *La Crosse Tribune,* and city directories and built an excellent reputation across the greater La Crosse community. Articles and obituaries refer repeatedly to the Norwegian roots of the Trane family. Certainly word of mouth recruited clients from Norwegian-American communities, but the company's Norwegian heritage was not overtly expressed in the firm's marketing.

Trane's son, Reuben (1886–1954), worked with his father in the plumbing business after completing high school and saved his earnings to attend the University of Wisconsin–Madison, where he earned a mechanical engineering degree in 1910. The younger Trane worked for a time with a Milwaukee machine tools firm, learning the business end of industrial production, before he rejoined his father in the plumbing business in La Crosse.

Together, the Tranes changed the focus of their company from plumbing to heating. James invented the low-pressure vapor heating system and was eager to promote and sell his product. Thus, in 1913, with a capitalization of $20,000 and a half dozen employees, father and son incorporated the Trane Company.

In 1916 they moved to Sixth Street in La Crosse, discontinued all plumbing activities, and concentrated on the production of the vapor heating system, specifically steam radiator traps and valves. Within three years they had outgrown their facility on Sixth Street, built a factory at Second and Cameron, and expanded their workforce to forty. Cold midwestern winters and World War I provided opportunities for the company to grow, for example, by manufacturing heating equipment for military barracks and war industrial plants.

The Tranes believed in utilizing top talent and cutting-edge engineering and business practices to grow their industry. In 1925, Reuben Trane introduced an innovative human engineering approach to the company—i.e., graduates were recruited from the strongest engineering programs in North America and

Figure 4. Jas. A. Trane & Co. located at 320 Pearl Street in 1891, La Crosse, Wisconsin. Courtesy of the La Crosse Public Library Archives.

then given detailed technical training on Trane products at the La Crosse location. The recruits received additional training as sales engineers in the company's field offices. In the early decades, the Trane enterprise was steered by family members, with Reuben as president and general manager; his father, James, as first vice president; and his brother-in-law, Frank Hood, as treasurer. Hood's vision and financial skills helped to propel the company forward to international markets, especially in Europe and Asia.

In 1923, Reuben invented the convector radiator utilizing a fin-and-tube coil, a new system demonstrated to be very efficient in heat transfer. Compared to the old cast iron radiators, the convector radiator was quiet and lightweight and appealed broadly to people in markets around the world. Business boomed in the 1920s and resulted in a new, larger factory in La Crosse. The Depression brought both strains and opportunities to the company. Determined to move forward, the father-son team pressed on by experimenting with new technologies.

Figure 5. With growth of the company, a new manufacturing plant was constructed on Second Street in La Crosse, shown here in the 1930s. Courtesy of the La Crosse Public Library Archives.

Figure 6. Reuben Trane, son of the founder, developed the company's human engineering program, recruiting top talent from the country's engineering schools. Reuben is pictured front row center. Courtesy of the La Crosse Public Library Archives.

The company began producing fans, for example, the first ones intended for Trane's own heating and ventilation systems. In 1931, Reuben discovered that his fin-and-tube coil system for heating could also be used for cooling. Thus, in the first years of the Great Depression, the Trane air conditioning industry was born, a game changer for the company. Reciprocating and centrifugal refrigeration compressors went into production—specifically, the Turbovac water chiller in 1938, the forerunner of large commercial air conditioning systems.

With the onset of the Second World War, the Trane Company shifted its production in full support of the war effort. By that time, there were 1,500 employed in the La Crosse plant. Reuben Trane played an active part in the local Liberty loan campaign. He was also known to work long hours alongside his engineers to bring new technologies into service. Trane engineers developed a method of brazing thin sheets of aluminum to make military aircraft lighter by one-third at half the cost of former production. They developed the first all-aluminum aircraft radiator for liquid-cooled engines, equipment to help prevent ice formation on airplane wings, and the technology to cool airplane cabins. They pioneered the distillation of seawater for drinking and manufactured the technologies to heat and cool warships and war production plants.

After the war, Reuben led the development of mechanical refrigeration for railroad freight cars, a cooling technology later built into passenger cars, trucks, buses, and truck-trailer refrigerated vehicles. The Trane Company moved into the atomic age by providing heat exchangers in atomic plants, first supplying those at Hanford, Washington, and Oak Ridge, Tennessee. In 1954, the company dedicated its Trane Research and Testing Laboratory, known as the House of Weather Magic, with a focus on atomic energy and the space race. Trane provided technology to the lunar rover in the 1970s.

In the company's first decades, Reuben Trane and brother-in-law Frank Hood were visionary in their plans for international markets. As early as 1927, Trane had twenty-three offices in the United States supplemented by offices in London, Tokyo, and Shanghai and factories in the United States and Canada. By 1945, there were sixty-six Trane offices in the United States with 200 sales engineers and a much broader global presence. Each branch office was staffed with top-notch engineers with training in sales, graduates of Reuben's training program in La Crosse. The company did not install equipment, unlike its competitors, but focused on innovation, testing, production, and marketing. A series of acquisitions and mergers through the years resulted in the creation of Trane Technologies in 2020, now with headquarters in Dublin, Ireland. Trane Technologies is a global giant with manufacturing plants in more than twenty countries, sales in about 100 countries, and annual sales exceeding $8 billion. The Channel Tunnel, Washington Monument, Statue of Liberty, Kremlin, and Athens Olympic Sports Complex are among many public facilities cooled by Trane.

Still strongly associated with La Crosse, Wisconsin, Trane is one of America's great immigrant success stories. From roots in La Crosse, the Trane Company grew and thrived in a multicultural world, adapting quickly and aggressively to changing business environments. Ethnic roots were not overtly expressed in the Trane industry, but Trane family members were most certainly influenced by their Nordic roots, particularly in a region permeated by Norwegian norms and values.

James and Reuben Trane combined their technical genius with determination and business finesse. Today the company's motto is known and quoted globally: "It's hard to stop a Trane."

Ann Marie Legreid *earned her PhD and master's degree in historical geography from the University of Wisconsin–Madison. She is professor emerita of geography at the University of Central Missouri and has served in deanships at Shepherd University in Shepherdstown, West Virginia.*

NOTE

1. This essay borrows from the author's forthcoming article "'It's Hard to Stop a Trane': A Case Study of Norwegian-American Ingenuity and Identity" in *Norwegian American Essays* (Norwegian American Historical Association—Norway Chapter). In preparing the article, the author utilized the Trane collection held at the La Crosse Public Library Archives, La Crosse, Wisconsin.

WORKS IN PROGRESS

Norwegians in the Slave Trade

UNVEILING HIDDEN HISTORIES OF COLONIALISM AND ENSLAVEMENT

Per Ivar Hjeldsbakken Engevold and Kari Lie Dorer

Norwegian Americans commonly use the year 1825 to mark the beginning of Norwegian migration to the Americas. The fifty-two Norwegians who set sail on the sloop *Restauration* from Stavanger were to become a symbol of the mass exodus of Norwegians who journeyed to establish a new life in America. However, Norwegians were in the Americas nearly 200 years prior—as a part of the transatlantic slave trade. What brought them there? And how do their stories fit within Norwegian-American histories?

How the small state of Denmark-Norway became involved in the trade of enslaved peoples and colonization is a complicated story. Throughout the seventeenth, eighteenth, and nineteenth centuries, Norwegians and Danes participated in the trafficking of enslaved Africans. Nearly 100,000 enslaved people were transported on Danish ships from the trading forts in Africa to the European

Figure 1. An artistic rendering of the Danish West Indies by Danish painter Fritz Melbye. Circa 1850. Courtesy of Wikimedia Commons, https://commons.wikimedia.org/wiki/File:Danish_West_India_-_Fritz_Melbye.jpg.

possessions in the Caribbean. Although the volume of trade was a small fraction (about 1 percent) of the estimated 10 to 12 million people enslaved and forcefully transported from Africa, it is a sea of people with many gruesome fates. Research on this exploitation colonialism focuses largely on Denmark.

Although the stories about the Dano-Norwegian colonies haven't vanished entirely, there has been little overall representation of the Norwegian roles within the Danish colonial empire until more recently. The colonial era and that of the transatlantic slave trade have become a more frequent topic of Norwegian researchers. Despite this, it seems that this information has taken a long time to reach the Norwegian public. While the average Norwegian knows little about Norway's role in the transatlantic slave trade, Norwegian Americans know far less.

When Per Ivar's book *Nordmenn i slavefart* was published in 2022, Kari knew that it would pique the interest of an English-language readership. And it just so happened that she was preparing for a year-long research sabbatical to the former Danish West Indies to further explore this history. We enthusiastically connected and began a new project, building on Per Ivar's Norwegian publication. Per Ivar's Norwegian publication centers on the scholarship at his disposal from his desk in Norway, and Kari first translated and then expanded many areas during a sabbatical year filled with site visits, attending events, speaking with locals, and having access to many publications that are not found off island. Our interests, expertise, and contributions complement each other well, creating a robust exploration of this unsettling past.

Though Kari was solely based in the Caribbean, the book itself details the colonial encounters of Norwegians throughout Southeast Asia, West Africa, and the Caribbean. It begins with the establishment of the colonial empire and discusses the lives of enslaved people, commerce, and resistance and continues through emancipation. The book ends with a discussion of Norwegian colonial legacy and racism today. This book pushes our own understanding of Norwegian and Norwegian-American history and also Norwegian and American colonialism. It aims to provide the English-speaking community with a more honest, nuanced understanding of Norwegians' role in colonialism outside of its borders.

Tentatively titled *Norwegians in the Slave Trade,* the book explores Norwegians from every walk of life who were participants in the slave trade. These individuals were from all over Norway—and they included the wealthy and influential elite, as well as those who were told that instead of serving a life sentence in a workhouse in Norway, they were to board a ship. They each contributed to the colonization efforts by providing a needed trade (such as shipbuilding, rope making, commerce, etc.). Additionally, there were many who never ventured from Norway's borders but who profited from the sugar refineries or shipping industry.

The book is written for a general audience, and along with presenting the various roles Norwegians had in the transatlantic slave trade, it addresses how this involvement shaped the development of racism in Norway and how financial investment in it affected the Norwegian economy. It is a thorough overview of what is known about Norway's involvement in four parts of the world: Southeast Asia, West Africa, the Caribbean, and Northern Europe. It puts all the pieces tied to Norway and Norwegians together in a way that hasn't been done before.

By all accounts, this is a thin slice of history. It is also one largely left out of both Norwegian and Norwegian-American history. Neither of us encountered the history of Norwegian colonization outside of Norway's borders in our own undergraduate or graduate studies; it was one we sought out independently many years later. Our hope is that disseminating the facts of the Dano-Norwegian colonization and trade of enslaved Africans will make it easier for English readers to have access to and engage with this history. The contents of this book are difficult, but they are, at the same time, extremely important.

We are looking to find a publisher who can help give our work an appropriate platform. We will be completing the writing during summer 2024 and hope to find a publisher who can work with our timeline to have the book in print to be used as part of the wider discussion of Norwegian migration to the Americas in 2025.

Per Ivar Hjeldsbakken Engevold *is a Norwegian author and historian. He authored the books* Thor Heyerdahl og jakten på Atlantis *(Thor Heyerdahl and the hunt for Atlantis) in 2019 and* Nordmenn i slavefart *(Norwegians in the slave trade) in 2022.*

Kari Lie Dorer *serves as the King Olav V Chair in Scandinavian-American Studies, chair of the Norwegian Department, and director of Nordic Studies at St. Olaf College. She has coauthored* Sett i gang 1 *and* 2 *and is the project leader of Godt i gang. She is the English-language editor and cotranslator of the book* Muus vs. Muus: The Scandal that Shook Norwegian America.

The Kravik-Lokensgard Diaries

Solveig Zempel

Norwegian-American pastor Ole Lokensgard and his wife, Ellen Kravik Lokensgard, were inveterate diary keepers.[1] Their grandson David Hardy located and preserved fifteen of their diaries written between 1879 and 1888. Ten of these were Ellen's diaries and five were kept by Ole. Mr. Hardy brought these diaries to my attention, encouraged me to translate them into English, and subsequently placed the diaries in the archives of the Norwegian American Historical Association (NAHA). A scanned electronic copy of the diaries and my complete translation are also available in the NAHA archives.

The Kravik-Lokensgard diaries were written primarily in Norwegian and have not been transcribed into print. The original texts are only available by studying the handwritten diaries. Working with handwritten documents has many challenges. When writing letters, the writer is conscious of trying to make the text clear to another person, even though they may well have a shared history or memories that don't need explanation. In writing a diary, the writer is conscious only of herself as reader, and thus she need not worry about either clarity of handwriting or context.

Figure 1. Ole Lokensgard with grandchildren, circa 1929. Løkensgaard Family Papers, Norwegian American Historical Association, Northfield, Minnesota.

The excerpts presented here are my translations. The act of translation is also an act of interpretation. No matter how diligently the translator attempts to convey accurately the original meaning and mood, the translated text is the product of constant choice of words, of syntax, and even of punctuation. I trust that my translation conveys as accurately as possible the daily lives and emotions, as well as the distinctive style of writing, that Ellen and Ole used in their respective diaries.

Scholars as well as general readers are interested in private writing such as letters and diaries for many reasons. Early scholarship and publication of diaries tended to focus on those that tell a story of a famous life (usually a man's life) or of a famous moment and that tell it well—in other words, that exhibit literary features.[2] These are not the kinds of diaries, however, that Ellen and Ole kept. I think Elizabeth Hampsten says it best when she maintains that we read private writings such as letters and diaries in a quest for a sense of presence, to hear the voices of our predecessors speaking for themselves. She adds that private writings allow us to "retrieve a genuine history of people who so far have largely been unaccounted for."[3] I think this is especially true for immigrants who wrote in languages other than English and whose private (as well as public) writings have tended to be ignored not only by the general public but also by scholars. These ordinary writings produced in America in a language other than English provide a fascinating glimpse into the lives of our predecessors, giving us a sense of their presence while greatly enriching our understanding of the American experience.

Who Were Ellen and Ole?

Ellen Kravik was born in Koshkonong, Wisconsin, in 1860, the daughter of Halvor and Kristi Kravik, who had emigrated separately from Buskerud in Norway.[4] Ellen's mother came to America with her own mother in 1842 and spent the first winter in the Norwegian-American settlement of Koshkonong, after which they were employed as domestic workers in Madison, Wisconsin. Ellen's father came to America in 1843, also arriving in Koshkonong, where he found work on a farm. Though he was reputedly illiterate when he came to America, Halvor became proficient in both Norwegian and English after his arrival, and since he saw to it that not only his sons but also his daughters went to school well beyond the usual minimum, it appears that he valued education. In 1844, Halvor filed a claim to acquire forty acres of government land in section thirty-five of Christiania Township in Dane County. One year after they were married, Halvor and Kristi were able to move into a stone house on their forty acres, located about half a mile south of the East Koshkonong Church. This farmstead was known as Kravikhaugen, or Kravik Hill. Halvor and Kristi had seven children. The first three died in infancy, but the remaining four survived to adulthood. These were Lars Christian, Carl Martin (referred to as "Martin" in Ellen's diaries), Ellen Christine, and Marie Helene.

Ellen and her sister both attended Monona Academy, a Norwegian-American preparatory school that shared a building with Luther Seminary in Madison. While studying at Monona Academy in 1878–1879, Ellen met, fell in love with, and became engaged to Ole Lokensgard, who was a seminary student.

Ole and Ellen were married in the summer of 1881. Ellen bore five children, of whom only the second and third (Olaf and Camilla) survived infancy. She died of diphtheria shortly after giving birth to her fifth child in 1892.

The Lokensgard name can be spelled in several ways, including *Løkensgaard, Løkensgård,* and, using only English letters, *Lokensgaard* or *Lokensgard.* The American family now uses the latter.[5] Ole Lokensgard was born in Hallingdal, Norway, in 1854. In 1857, when he was two and a half years old, he emigrated to Minnesota with his parents, Ole and Helga, and older sister, Sigrid. After arriving in America, the family grew with the addition of brothers Mikkel, Knute, and Oluf and another sister, Olina. The family first lived in Red Wing and then farmed in Rice County, near Northfield. In 1861, the family traveled by wagon train to Dakota Territory, where they settled near Vermillion, in what is now South Dakota. However, they soon returned to Minnesota, settling in Nicollet County, near Saint Peter. Helga was left a widow in 1871, seven months before her youngest child, Olina, was born. Shortly after his father's death, Ole left for Decorah, Iowa, where he spent three years in preparatory school and then four years at Luther College. In 1878, he entered Luther Seminary in Madison, Wisconsin. As soon as Ole was ordained in 1881, he and Ellen were married and moved to Granite Falls, Minnesota, where he served both the Lutheran congregation in town and the larger rural Bergen congregation at Stony Run, as well as several other rural churches.

After Ellen's death, Ole married Anna Romtvedt, and they had nine children in addition to Olaf and Camilla. Ole served as pastor in several churches in southwestern Minnesota and was the first president of the Lutheran Normal School in Madison, Minnesota. He died in December of 1931.

The Norwegian-American Context

The Kravik and Lokensgard families took part in the massive relocation of Norwegians to the United States that occurred between 1825 and the 1920s. Though Ole was born in Norway, he came as a small child with his family, and Ellen was born in Wisconsin to parents who had immigrated as young adults. Thus, they are products of the immigration that took place in the 1840s and 1850s.[6]

The Koshkonong community in Wisconsin, where Ellen grew up, was a well-established Norwegian-American enclave. Located near Lake Koshkonong in eastern Dane and western Jefferson Counties, the Koshkonong area is even today strongly influenced by the immigration of Norwegians.

When the Lokensgard family settled in Nicollet County in Minnesota, they became part of a sizable Norwegian-American community. Norwegian churches were established in the area, and the Norwegian language was widely used. Though they no doubt interacted with "Americans" and other immigrant groups, the Norwegians in these areas had also created a quite self-contained community.

Ole went off to school in Decorah, Iowa, a strongly Norwegian-American community, and studied at one of the early Norwegian-American educational institutions, finishing both preparatory school and college at Luther College. The college at that time was essentially devoted to preparing young men for the seminary. At Luther, his schooling was carried out primarily in Norwegian, though he also studied English and German, as well as Latin, Greek, and Hebrew. Just before Ole finished at Luther, the Norwegian Synod established its seminary in Madison, Wisconsin, so that young Norwegian Americans could be trained as pastors there instead of at the Missouri Lutheran Seminary in Saint Louis. Madison was an urban area and, hence, not quite so strongly Norwegian as the Koshkonong, Decorah, and Nicollet County settlements that Ellen and Ole had previously experienced. Nonetheless, their schooling continued to be carried out in Norwegian, and the people they associated with were still largely fellow Norwegian Americans.

Monona Academy, a coeducational high school, was founded in 1876, shortly before Ellen studied there, and closed in 1881, a mere five years later. Monona was one of a number of such academies established by Norwegian Americans to educate their youth using mostly Norwegian as the language of instruction and including a strong religious element in the curriculum. Luther Seminary was located in Madison from 1876 to 1888, and the academy and the seminary were housed together in the old Farwell mansion on Spaight Street, formerly the Soldiers' Orphans' Home.[7] It was not unusual for academy students to become engaged to seminarians, as happened to both Ellen and her sister.

When Ellen and Ole settled in Granite Falls, Minnesota, after their marriage, they once again were in a community strongly marked by fellow Norwegian Americans. While Koshkonong and Madison, Wisconsin, Nicollet County, Minnesota, and Decorah, Iowa, were all older, established communities when Ole and Ellen lived there, the area around Granite Falls in Yellow Medicine and adjoining Chippewa Counties in Minnesota had only recently moved from frontier status. Indeed, the railroad had arrived in Granite Falls in 1878, a mere three years before Ellen and Ole. When Ole went on his missionary trips to Dakota Territory, he encountered Norwegian Americans living in settler conditions on the frontier, which was moving steadily westward.

After Ole accepted the call to Granite Falls, he and Ellen lived in town, where he had a congregation. However, his largest congregation was rural, and he served a widespread parish requiring frequent trips to Palmer Creek and Stony Run. He describes holding confirmation classes in granaries and church services in schoolhouses, as in these entries from his 1885 and 1884 diaries.

Tuesday, July 14, 1885

Drove to Stony Run to confirmation. They were all there, we are still meeting in Samson's granary. It is not going so well for some of them. Drove home again in the evening. Mr. Otis had been here with hay, and threw most of the hay down outside of the barn. I dug up some of it. Hard job.

Saturday, December 27, 1884

Jensen came with his boy and put up the storm windows. I drove to Palmer Creek, where there were church services in the schoolhouse by Sønsteli's. Stayed for dinner at Martin Pederson's. Got home in good time in the evening.

Eventually, churches were erected both for the rural Bergen congregation and the town congregation in Granite Falls. The primary language of both the town and the rural congregations was Norwegian.

A Note about Diaries

Diaries are a conventional form of writing. For example, diarists often address their diaries directly as "Dear Diary" or "My Book." Conventional topics include weather, lists of tasks accomplished, state of health, and expressions of personal feelings. Diaries differ from letters, as Steven Stowe points out, by usually being contained between covers, thus resembling a book rather than a conversation.[8] The popularity of printed diaries probably reinforced conventions such as recording of weather and keeping of financial records, and the restricted space created constraints on the amount of information that could be recorded for any given day.[9] The diaries of Ellen and Ole, written in standard American pocket diaries, for the most part follow the conventions of diary writing and clearly are affected by the limited space available for each entry in the printed diaries. However, they were also able to transcend these restrictions when so inclined. For example, Ellen might write up the side and around the edges of the page, and once she even pasted in an extra flap of paper in order to continue the entry for that day. Both Ellen and Ole sometimes ran an entry for one day over into the space allotted to the next, thus privileging the account for that day. Both might also write the entry for a particular date at a later time, thus giving a retrospective view, and sometimes days and even long periods of time are simply left blank. Ellen kept her first diary in a composition book, giving her space for longer and more detailed entries than her other diaries.

As Orm Øverland points out, immigrant letters generally give a reliable account of material conditions.[10] This is likely true of diaries as well. There is not much reason to doubt the accuracy of reports of washing, ironing, baking, visiting, and so on. They are almost certainly, however, not complete, and in that way they may be unreliable. Births, deaths, and marriages, common fodder for family letters, are also frequently recorded in diaries and are certainly found in those of Ellen and Ole. They also note their daily tasks, mention visits and parties, and give information about their families, friends, neighbors, and parishioners. Journeys are described in some detail. Their diaries contain comments on religion, politics, and world and local events and reveal their passage through life, from student life to courtship and marriage, moving to a new home in the west, and daily duties as housewife, pastor, and parents.

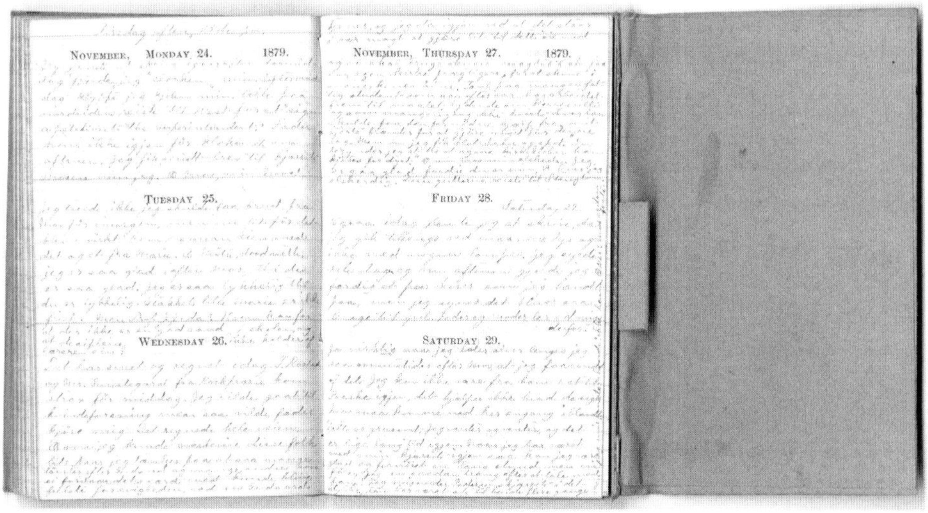

Figure 2. Ellen Kravik Lokensgard's diary. Note how she writes as much as possible on the paper, including in the margins. Courtesy of the Norwegian American Historical Association, Northfield, Minnesota.

Øverland also notes that "individual texts gain a greater significance when read as parts of a larger text."[11] Having diaries from both Ellen and Ole provides a female and a male perspective on the same events, enhancing our ability to interpret them. Other public and private sources, such as immigrant letters from the period, and what we know of historical conditions in that place and time can also help us interpret these texts and enable us better to capture that "sense of presence" that Hampsten mentions. Our understanding of the lives of immigrants is greatly enriched when we have access to all of these types of texts.

Diaries are more likely than letters to contain introspection, to reveal the writer's innermost thoughts and feelings, while letters typically report on events in greater detail and contain more news. In their diaries, Ellen and Ole frequently express their profound love for each other and use the diaries as outlets for their emotions. Both write heartrending descriptions of the illness and death of their one-year-old son, and Ellen reveals the problems of her first, somewhat difficult, pregnancy. One day's entry that reports (in Norwegian) on the weather and the Ladies' Aid meeting ends with the words "O Dear Dear Dear Dear" written in scrawling handwriting and in English in contrast to the rest of the entry. Reading this, we certainly sense that she was emotionally and physically distressed. Of course we would like to know much more. Was she suffering from false labor? Was she terrified of the upcoming birth? Or was she just unhappy with the domestic help?

In addition to revealing thoughts and feelings, diaries can also provide rich descriptions of memorable events. The Kravik-Lokensgard diaries, for example, describe public events such as the lectures by Kristofer Janson and Bjørnstjerne Bjørnson in lively detail.[12] Ellen describes these lectures in vivid detail in lengthy entries in her 1880 and 1881 diaries.

> ***Thursday, March 18, 1880***
>
> Early today I got an unexpected letter from my Mosen.[13] He has heard K. Janson and writes to ask me to go and hear him. I don't know how it will go. Everyone up there has liked him so very much. Well, I got to hear Kr. Janson too, and just as Mos assured me, I do not regret it, and not Father either. He said nothing yesterday, and I did not think he would go. I am sure that he would not have gone if Mosa's letter had not come, Mos wanted so much for me to hear, and Father thought then that he had better take me up on account of Mos. I regret most that Mother could not come along. Many of the more enlightened from far and near were there. Hannah Ottesen was there as well as the Methodist pastor who wanted to give a lecture before Janson came, but that did not get anywhere. I came inevitably to think of Prof. Anderson's talks. He did not want anyone in the audience to have sinful tobacco in his mouth while they were in the house of God. But—suddenly! All heads turn! In came Kr. Janson! The most handsome Norwegian I have ever seen. He smiled to all sides, while he went forward.
>
> ***Friday, March 19, 1880***
>
> Dundas came behind in his best mood.[14] We had to wait a little while before he stepped up, then Dundas came, bowed so he was almost bent double, screwed his face into the most laughable

grimace, and cried out "Ladies and gentlemen." However that was all the English he used. He introduced Janson and ended with "come out on the floor with hops and leaps, kick your foot to the sky and swing yourself around—Kristoffer Janson." Janson came smiling from Dundas's "stump approach." He recited "How the Mountain was Clad" (by Bjørnson) in Landsmaal and then developed his talk from it, about how we should all help to heal Norway's flaws, in other words, clothe the mountain. He described conditions both here and in Norway splendidly and many times so comically that—in spite of the Methodist pastor's admonitions they could not hold back from a "cheer." And old men were so enthusiastic that they burst out from time to time "in spite of everything." *Yes it is true*! I liked it so much, my Mos. . . . A sewing machine salesman was here and left a machine for tomorrow. It is "Amarikan." Oh I love my Mosen so much, it is so lovely out this evening, clear and starry, moonlit and mild. Now soon my Mosen will come. . . . We are thinking of going to Madison tomorrow . . . and then we can hear Bjørnson at the same time.[15] Then I will have much to tell my book.

Wednesday, January 5, 1881

Yesterday afternoon we left. Everything went well on the journey. When we got to Madison we stopped first at Seim's, where we unloaded. There we got coffee together with Prof. Lynne from Northfield. . . . Everything was as usual there, and when they remembered that I naturally wanted to hear Bjørnson they all burst out laughing. In the evening I went with my Mosen up to the City Hall, where we were going to hear him. The hall was already half full when we came in, but we got seats in the first row so that we could easily look Bjørnson in the eye when he appeared. There were many from Stoughton and different people from around here. Prof. Stub came soon and together with him Miss Stub and Torgrimson, Mrs. Ylvisaker and Olaf Stub. We waited half an hour, and in that time the hall was almost filled. But———then there was a clapping and a stamping of feet, we turned around and saw—Bjørnson! Smiling and bowing, I saw him for the first time. Lightly as a youth, he went forward while the applause continued. After him came Dr. Dundas from Cambridge and Senator Johnson of Madison. When he came up on the stage, the noise began again, but Bjørnson interrupted them with a smile and a bow. Oh what a fine man he is, when he throws back his head (which is his manner). He is of medium height, well built, his hair stands boldly up in a shock, which never fell out of its place, his eyes are dark poet's eyes, just exactly the kind of eyes one can read love in, and his voice——————oh it was music! I have never heard such a voice. Full, clear, and fervent. He started by declaiming his own poem "Olav Tryggvason" and it was beautiful. When I went home again it seemed as though I heard a voice above me repeating "Comes not Olav Tryggvason?" Later he went on to describe "The ghost of the Viking spirit" and then he went into many different things, mostly historical. He described very well the differences between the 3 Nordic kingdoms. He did not mention Christianity, so I don't think anyone could regret having heard him. I would not have missed it for anything. Gjevre said "when I saw this man and heard him, then I could have wept at the thought that he has gone from us, that he is a freethinker." I think the same. That evening, when I went to bed, it seemed to me that I could see so much farther and higher, and when my thoughts met with God it was with a heartfelt prayer for this man, that he would come to praise the giver of his wonderful gifts. God does not disdain any sincere prayer. Oh, if only Bjørnson were a Christian! . . . The next morning I said farewell to everyone . . . and went with Mosen up to town for a while, and then we went home. It was such a fun trip that I had with my Mosen.

Rebecca Hogan contends that diaries "do not privilege 'amazing' over 'ordinary' events in terms of scope, space, or selection."[16] Robert A. Fothergill agrees and maintains that "in diary after diary [historical] events float by like rumours."[17] To a certain extent, I believe this is true. However, in the Kravik-Lokensgard diaries, some historical events are indeed mentioned and commented on, sometimes in considerable detail. The assassination of President Garfield and their reaction to it is reported; elections are noted, as are public celebrations, church politics, and local political matters. For example, in her diary entry for 4 July 1881, Ellen writes of the Garfield assassination, "Yesterday we got the sad news that our president, Garfield, was shot by a coward, and that there is no hope for his life. It is strange how something like this goes to the heart. We know him only by name, but we know that the government of our country lies in his hands (such cannot of course be said of a republic, but you, my book, understand me well enough). He is like our father and when we also know him as an honorable, good, and faithful man, then—our hearts are turned to melancholy and all of America grieves." Ole notes an election in one of his diary entries and states that he "voted straight Republican."

While diaries are not particularly useful in learning new facts about historical events—they are both too cryptic and too personal for that—what we can learn from them is how these individuals led their daily lives and how they felt about events and people. In addition, the diaries of Ellen and Ole can help us dispel some stereotypes of Norwegian Americans—for example, that they are reserved about expressing their feelings, especially their feelings of love.

We might also wonder what counts as "amazing" as opposed to "ordinary." Ole's diary for 4 and 5 August 1885 describes a dramatic event. The entry for Tuesday reads: "Dry and chilly weather. Sent 4 Chinese lanterns to Marie. At supper time the Arabs Elias and Johannes came. A whole mob followed after them, but they stayed out in the street and wanted to get them when they came back out. But the Arabs stayed here for supper, slept in the barn for the night. They were very well behaved. They sang in the evening." He follows up the next day with: "The Arabs left as soon as they had gotten breakfast. I have read in Milton today and have now begun reading about Rowland Hill. In the evening we sang. Miss Larson came this evening too. Mr. Lockrem from Goodhue was there. Everyone is asking about the Arabs. Bis bought a ring from them. Bis has gone to bed, now I am going too."[18]

I turned eagerly to Ellen's diary for the same date to get her version of this eventful visit. She surely prepared the food for these unexpected visitors, and according to Ole, she bought a ring from them. Normally her diary would mention those who came to visit, shared meals with them, and stayed the night. In her diary for that Tuesday she writes: "Today I have washed, and it was a big washing. Now it is thundering so I will probably have to go out after the clothes." That's it. She continues on Wednesday with: "Today I ironed everything but the shirts." She does not mention the Arabs, the mob, or the purchase of the ring. Had I access only to Ellen's diary, I would never have known about these intriguing visitors.

In addition to being often cryptic and incomplete in the original, we must be cognizant that published diaries have been transcribed and edited and sometimes, as with the Kravik-Lokensgard diaries, transformed through translation from one language to another. Furthermore, even in working with collections of diaries such as these where we have original manuscripts, we need to "ask questions about [the collection's] completeness and inclusiveness."[19] In many of Ellen's and Ole's diaries, days if not months can go by with no entries made. We cannot know what was going on in their lives in those periods. I have fifteen diaries from Ellen and Ole, but I have no diaries for some years, especially from Ole. Can I assume that no diary was kept in that year, or has the diary been lost? Without some kind of evidence, such as a notation that "I kept no diary last year," I cannot know this. I have been told by a Lokensgard family member that Ole continued to keep diaries after Ellen's death and that at least some of these are extant, but I have not seen any of these later diaries. Does this matter? It may, depending on what assumptions or conclusions are being drawn from the material in the diaries. We must also be careful about what we surmise about all those events and feelings that the diarist may have suppressed.

In order to be read by someone other than the intended audience, diaries must be collected and preserved. We can never know, of course, what is contained in those diaries that are no longer available to us. Questions to pose of all personal or private texts are why, how, and by whom have they been saved? What, if anything, has been added or deleted, and why?

As David Fitzpatrick reminds us in his study of immigrant letters, we simply cannot know what has been lost or suppressed. Therefore, we must be exceedingly cautious in making claims about what is "typical" or "average." Those private writings—both diaries and letters—that have been saved are in fact likely not typical.[20] I would certainly hesitate to make such a claim for the diaries I have worked with.

Jennifer Sinor, in her study of "ordinary writing," claims that diaries are more difficult to read and categorize than other types of texts because of the distinct kind of writing found in them. The single most important characteristic of the diary, according to her, is its dailiness.[21] Laurel Thatcher Ulrich agrees and reminds us that it is in this exhaustive, repetitious dailiness that the real power of a diary lies.[22] We certainly see this in Ellen's and Ole's diaries.

Stowe gives some helpful tips on how to make sense of texts such as diaries and letters.[23] He reminds us that although diaries and letters are immediate, familiar, and comfortable to read, they are not as simple as they first seem. Though both letters and diaries seem to be private kinds of writing, they are always, he maintains, written for an audience. Understanding just who the implied or understood audience is makes a difference in how we interpret the text.

Lynn Bloom argues that, while those diaries written with a public audience in mind can stand alone, those that were written for the writer's eyes only, those we have been referring to as "ordinary" diaries, require painstaking efforts at reconstruction if their content and context are to be at all clear.[24] Although many scholars claim that no diary is truly intended to be read by the writer alone, we might agree that any diary to be published will require the addition of extra material to provide clarity in content and context. I am confident that Ole and Ellen did not imagine the publication of their diaries; however, they often shared their diaries with each other at the time of writing. Sometimes they even wrote in each other's diaries. Ellen also reports sharing her diary with her younger sister. In one of her last diaries, Ellen mentions its usefulness as a record of her life for her children. These diaries, thus, do indeed have an implied and understood audience beyond the writers themselves. Just the fact that these small books were carefully preserved indicates that perhaps they were intended to be read by others.

Marilyn Ferris Motz notes that diaries enable us to see the writers as engaging their environment and one another in an active interchange of ideas and provide us with insight into the ways in which they interpreted and responded to their immediate, as well as their national and international, milieus.[25] As Arthur Ponsonby says, "[Diaries] are better than novels, more accurate than histories, and . . . more dramatic than plays."[26] Anthony Quinn writes eloquently on the importance of diaries, calling them "a wonderful window on the past."[27] The diaries of Ellen and Ole Lokensgard are all of that and provide a goldmine of interesting insights into their lives and into their Norwegian-American context.

About the Kravik-Lokensgard Diaries

Both Ellen and Ole were habitual diary keepers, and the diaries in this collection start when they were a courting couple and continue through their first seven years of marriage and his first seven years as a parish pastor. Ellen's diaries cover the ten years from 1879 to 1888, with a few entries from December of 1878, though some years are quite incomplete when she fails to write for long periods of time. Ole's five diaries include all or part of the years 1879–1880, 1883, 1884, 1885, and 1887.

Ellen's first diary is written in a composition book; her other diaries and all of Ole's are in one-year pocket diaries with dates preprinted and small blocks allocated to each day. The covers of the diaries are decorated, and the books are quite attractive. These books are small (most are three by five inches), and there is space on each page for from one to four entries, giving from one inch to about four inches of space to write in. Handwriting is consequently very tiny and occasionally illegible. Personal names can be particularly difficult to decipher. Ellen's hand is mostly clear, though her capital *L* and capital *S* are indistinguishable. Ole's handwriting is more difficult to read. He often seemed to be writing in a hurry, and sometimes he wrote with what appears to be a purple pencil (and sometimes on a moving train), which further complicates deciphering his writing.

Figure 3. Outside cover of the diaries used by Ole and Ellen. Courtesy of the Norwegian American Historical Association, Northfield, Minnesota.

Ellen and Ole often use a rather telegraphic writing style, as is forced by limited space. Ellen's entries are generally clear and straightforward, while Ole's are sometimes couched in more complex syntax and use abstract vocabulary. The diaries are mostly written in correct standard Norwegian. Both writers include occasional words, sentences, and phrases in English, but only Ellen writes slightly longer passages in English, especially in her school years. As we would expect, most of their diary entries are written as narratives. "It was cold today," "I had toothache all day," "Went to Stony Run," and so on. However, quite often they address each other directly, almost as though the diary is functioning as a sort of conversation with the other person, as in "Bis, I am home with you now," or "Dear Bis, I love you," or "Many sweet goodnights Mosen from your Bissus." Occasionally they would exchange diaries to read and even write comments in them. As is typical for diarists, they sometimes refer to their diaries as "my book," and Ellen addresses her diary directly when she writes: "My book, I have neglected you shamefully." Besides simple narration and addressing each other or their book, they also directly address God at times with thanks and prayers.

Ellen and Ole were both given to using nicknames for each other. Early in their courtship, Ellen refers to Ole as "Nenemooska." Later she shortens *Nenemooska* to *Mos* and variations such as *Mosen* or *Mosi.* Ole uses the same term for her, as well as *Bis, Bissen, Bissus,* and once *Bisbillibis.* Before their first child is born, they refer to him as "the Nene," presumably from their old nickname *Nenemooska.* When their son is born, they rarely refer to him by his name, Olaf Herman, but rather call him "Tubbi" or "Snuppen" and "Dutten" or "Dutti," which is baby talk for the Norwegian *Gutten,* meaning "the boy." They use some of the same nicknames for their second son. Ellen and Ole also occasionally write in baby talk in the narrative as when they write *Doodneth* for the exclamation *Goodness!*

One of the most common themes in these diaries is that of love. Their diaries reveal that Ellen and Ole loved each other deeply, and they express their love for each other freely and often. For example, every year at Easter time, both remark on the anniversary of their engagement, which happened on Easter Eve of 1879. References to their physical love for each other, though sometimes oblique, can also be found. For example, they both write about how sweet it is to exchange kisses, and they use the code word *rats* for kisses during their courting days. Ellen writes passages such as "Today I have not done much more than cuddle with my Mosen," or "Mosen was so scampy tonight," or "Bislen is thinking about the bed, I believe." Ole writes such lines as "Oh, wouldn't it be nice, Mos—to go to bed every night with my own dear Mos, and stay all night, and have fun too, you bet, so our bed needs to be a strong one" and later "I stayed in bed for a long time today. It was so good to lie with my Bissen."

Religious sentiments are frequently expressed in the diaries. These are often found on significant dates, such as the New Year or religious holidays, or at times of grief, such as on the death of their first child at the age of one. Just as an example, on 31 December 1884, Ellen wrote, "The dear Lord God be thanked for this year and all good." Ole's entry for the same date is very similar: "God has blessed me richly in the past year. His name be praised!"

As one might expect, given Ole's profession, church life is a major theme in the diaries. Both Ellen and Ole report on church services, subjects of sermons, and activities of the Ladies' Aid, where Ellen often served as an officer. She also assisted in fundraising activities, such as "sociables" where food was served and the group, often 100 or more, played games and auctioned items the women had made. Ellen was active in the Ladies' Aid when she was living at home in 1879–1880, as well as later taking on such duties as pastor's wife.

Norwegian Lutherans were engaged in numerous controversies during the years Ellen and Ole kept their diaries. Some of the controversies alluded to in the diaries were theological in nature, such as the debate over predestination, which hinged on whether salvation belonged only to those elected by God or to those who had faith. There were also controversies over church politics, some of which were interrelated with the theological disputes. Laypeople and clergy did not always agree on issues, and many of the controversies were also intertwined with difficult personalities. Both Ellen and Ole are disturbed by and comment on church politics and on the controversies over predestination, conversion, and other matters that raged among Norwegian-American Lutherans of the time. They confide gossip about various pastors to their diaries as well—for example, the difficulties of Pastor Bernt Julius Muus and his wife and a report about two St. Olaf professors who were fired for kissing female students against their will.[28]

Both Ellen and Ole comment, sometimes in passing and sometimes in more detail, about elections. On Tuesday, 6 November 1883, Ole reports that he "went up and cast my vote 'straight Republican.'" As noted above, Ellen comments in some detail about the election and, later, the assassination of President Garfield. In addition to national events, Ole and Ellen also mention local events, such as murders, fires, scandals, and criminal activity. As is typical of diaries, much is left to the reader's imagination, as the writer has no need to elaborate on the details. An entry may reflect the writer's feelings about an event rather than describing the event.

Lectures, concerts, and other cultural activities are described, sometimes in detail, other times only mentioned in passing. As we have seen, Ellen's diary gives vivid descriptions of the visits and lectures of both Kristofer Janson and Bjørnstjerne Bjørnson. Ellen and Ole describe these events in colorful detail, and their diaries also give insight into their feelings and reactions to the events.

Ellen and Ole were avid readers, and they often mention books they are reading. These range from classic and popular literature to magazines, poetry, history, church periodicals, and other religious writings. Ole, naturally, reads much that is connected to his professional life, such as works of theology and church controversies. Ellen also reports reading religious writings, such as Luther's sermons and church magazines. Both read an eclectic selection of secular works in English and Norwegian, and Ole reads books in German as well. Ellen and Ole often read the same poetry and fiction. They report reading aloud to each other and frequently give each other books as gifts.

Accounts of daily life are common in these diaries. In Ellen's diaries, washing and ironing, cooking and cleaning, weaving, quilting, sewing, and doing fancywork (decorative needlework) are frequently mentioned. In November of 1879 Ellen describes, for example, how she feels when her family gets a number of ducks from Dr. Dundas, and then she and her mother have to deal with them. She writes: "Pluck and pull, pull and pluck. I am so sick of it, I smell only the smell of ducks and there is just feathers and blood wherever I turn. We have cleaned 14 today. I am longing so for my Mosen, oh how I long. I am so tired and sick of this that I have to go to bed." Then she grumbles, "And when I don't have my Mos with me then it's no use to sit up or go to bed either."

Ellen's diaries show that she visits other women and helps those who are sick or in need, and they visit and assist her in turn. Ole's diaries describe his participation in childcare and household chores, as well as his work as a pastor, preparing sermons, reading with the confirmands, preaching, administering communion, and holding funerals. Both often comment on what the other is doing. Ole might mention that Ellen has been doing fancywork, has entered her items at the fair, and so on, while she will report that he held services at this or that location or officiated at a wedding. The Lokensgards gave and attended parties, sometimes describing these in detail. At one of their first parties, for members of the congregation and neighbors, they report serving beer, wine, and popcorn. Ellen's mother's birthday was on 1 January, so in addition to celebrating the New Year, they celebrated her birthday. Ellen reports that her mother served them all a glass of wine before breakfast in honor of the occasion.

Travel is another common theme in the diaries. When they are living in Madison, they often describe travel back and forth to Ellen's home in Koshkonong. Sometimes Ellen's father comes to Madison with the horse and wagon to get them, at other times they take the train to Stoughton and are met there. When they are living in Granite Falls, Ole travels about the prairie visiting his rural congregation and parishioners by buggy in the summer and cutter in the winter. He often reports taking the train from Granite Falls to Montevideo and back, a trip of less than fifteen miles. Ole describes in some detail several longer trips to church conventions or missionary trips to Dakota Territory, where he preaches, baptizes, marries, and administers communion to Norwegian-American settlers.

Ellen also makes several trips from Granite Falls. She visits her family in Koshkonong and travels by herself to Dakota to visit friends. In their diaries they describe the landscape, the people they meet, and the vagaries of travel by train, stage, buggy, or wagon. When Ole is away from home, Ellen expresses loneliness and some anxiety and often spends the night at the home of friends or has someone come and stay with her. When Ellen is away, Ole writes of his longing for her and reports getting most of his meals from neighbors. Frequently, Ellen accompanies him to his rural parish and to Synod meetings in other towns, and then they often stay overnight at one home or another. Comments in their diaries describe some of the discomforts encountered, such as unpleasant companions in bed—namely, bedbugs!

In their diaries, Ellen and Ole make frequent references to their families. They report on letters sent and received, on visits to and from family members, and on activities of family members and their personalities. Both Ellen and Ole depict her father as typically Norwegian in his stubbornness. Neighbors, parishioners, and townspeople are also mentioned in the diaries. Ellen and Ole describe who they visit and who comes to visit them and talk about marriages, births, deaths, and other significant events pertaining to their friends and acquaintances. They describe in detail such celebrations as the Fourth of July, Seventeenth of May, and especially Christmas and Easter.[29] At Christmas, they give long lists of the gifts that each of them received and gave and from and to whom.

Weather is of course important to both Ellen and Ole and is typical fodder for diaries. Ole often travels about by horse and buggy on the prairie, and naturally they report storms, snow, unusual cold and heat, and the changing of the seasons. In the diaries written while they are still in Wisconsin, Ellen frequently refers to "tobacco weather." Tobacco was one of the major crops raised by Norwegian-American farmers in that area of Wisconsin, and naturally having appropriate weather for the crop was important and thus worthy of noting in her diary. In the winter, they often report on sleighing conditions, as good sleighing conditions made for much easier travel.

The diaries of Ellen and Ole Lokensgard make fascinating reading. Below are some examples to whet your appetite and give a sense of their writing. These brief excerpts are chosen from three periods of their life: school, courtship, and farm life (1880), marriage and parsonage life (1883), and family and congregation (1887). So that the reader can get a sense of how each of them reacted to the same events, the following samples of Ole's and Ellen's diaries are from the same dates.

Diary Excerpts

Here are excerpts from Ole's 1880 diary:

> ***Tuesday, January 20, 1880***
>
> My Mos, perhaps I will sit with you tomorrow evening. Oh, it will be so much fun. Yes, I am going to my Mosen, if I can study while I am with her, then I will be so much cleverer, when I get back again. Doodneth, my own dear Mos, I long for you. . . . I have been sitting here alone all evening, there is a double chess game going on . . . and Storli is in there watching the progress of the

battle, many others are there too. I have thought and worked on a sermon this evening. I am tired, now I will sleep. Oh, how fun it will be to come home to my Mosen in a few days, I will be so clever afterward, my Mosen. Good night, darling Mos.

Wednesday Morning, January 21, 1880

Doodneth Mot mine, now I am ready to travel to you. Oh how good it will be. O. Larson spoke yesterday about going along, but today he says that he cannot. Very well, I shall have fun with Mot mine. I will sleep with my Mosen then. Now it is almost 10 o'clock, and I will go over to meet Marie and get a letter from her to my Mosen, and then carry it off to town, and then to the depot, and then to Stoughton and then to——Oh my doodneth, Mot mine. I will hurry home to my Mosen. My Mos, now I am coming soon, beloved Mos. By-by until we see each other, my dearest Ellen.

Kravik, Thursday, January 22, 1880

Oh, how well I rested last night! Slept with my Mosen all night, until long into the day I lay with my Mosen. It is so very good once again to be at home with my own beloved Mos. It is snowing and storming today. Yesterday it rained during the whole trip from Stoughton. I walked the whole way and as I came past Lien's my Mosen was there, but I didn't know it. I got home and found that my Mosen was . . . at Ladies Aid. I thought that it was too bad that I hadn't gone in there, but as soon as my Mosen came, doodneth, I got to kiss her and sit with her and last night, my Mot, it was good to sleep in your embrace, and lie in your arms. Now my Mosen came down and kissed me, we will have breakfast, and I will get to sit with my Mosen. [Ellen][30] My beloved Mos! Let the storm rage and the wind howl "we won't pay any attention." It felt so good when I lay in your arms my darling. Oh how beloved you are to me Mos and how good it is that you came to your Mos now. So very good it was,—and therefore I will kiss you all the time my Mosen. My Mos what are you thinking about now. Perhaps about whether your Mos will soon come and kiss you. Now I am coming my Mos.

Friday Morning, January 23, 1880

It is so beautiful out today, it has frozen so there is a little sleighing conditions. We had such a good time last night, Mosen and I, "doodneth, I guess he can" said Mos, my Mos. Oh how good it will be when my Mos and I can live together all the time, doodneth how much fun we shall have sometimes. We have fun now, too, you bet, but we only play now. Yes, my Mos, you are so heedlessly, willfully good to lie with. I hear that my Mosen is getting dressed up in the loft, now she will soon come. Breakfast is waiting for us, it is past 9 o'clock.

Sunday, January 25, 1880

It is so beautiful out, a little foggy but sunshine. My Mosen is up in the loft, getting dressed. Yesterday we went out driving, we had Flora and the cutter. Up in the road by Vehus we tipped the cutter and we and everything that was in it tipped out into the snow pile. Nothing broke. My Mos was not afraid either, she laughed and thought it was fun. We were in Cambridge and then we got the mail in Christiania—"Kirketiden"[31] reviewed "Altes und Neues"[32] but thought that there is no real disagreement between the teachers Schmidt and Walther, but that the whole thing is a misunderstanding. If only that were true! But I hope that our God will be victorious again this time. Now my Mos came and kissed me. Mosen kisses me now and then, you see. Now it is breakfast, I will go up to Mos and sit with her at the table. I am with Mos everywhere now.

Here are excerpts from Ellen's 1880 diary, recounting many of the same incidents from her point of view:

Tuesday, January 20, 1880

It has been such remarkably lovely weather today, one has to be astonished to have it so mild in the middle of winter. I am working on sewing Marie's dress. Father was up to Simon after little Fanny today, she had gotten lost yesterday, and we were completely worried about our little pet.

Wednesday, January 21, 1880

Doodneth, Mot, who could have thought of such a thing? Not me, my Mosen. We were at Ladies Aid at Lien's. The first table setting ate, then Gunnild Lien came in, and stammered something to me about someone being outside, but she had no doubt heard wrong. "Who is outside, is it the Jonsaas boys?" I said. I had heard that they were at Martin's, and were going to come to us. But she said "They say that Løkensgaard went down there." Could I believe my ears? Mosen *mine*! Had he come? Oh Mos you cannot imagine how happy I was. I ran out but my Mos had already left. He did not know that I was there and wanted to hurry home. He had walked from Stoughton all the way. I could not stay at Lien's. I ran home as fast as I could. Mos came out and met me and how happy I was that once again I could lay my head on his breast. The teachers had gone to a meeting in Decorah and weren't coming back before Monday. Marie is well. I will now be able to sleep in my Mosa's arms. Doodneth.

Thursday, January 22, 1880

Oh how well I slept last night with my Mosen! But he was so wild, my little Mosen, it is a long time since he was with his Mosen. I did not think this was so bad, and after we had a little scuffle, then we slept so well, we two, Mos and I, you bet! Father and Mother had to wait a little for us, but they did not take offense at that. It has been snowing and blowing all day, but there is still water standing from the rain yesterday, so it is not possible to use the sleigh. I wonder how little Marie is? In the evening. Now I will just write a little with Mosa's pen. . . . This afternoon Mos has written and I have crocheted. Doodneth how fun it was to sit with my Mosen and work. . . . Mosen does not want to have a "cease-fire" tonight either, it looks like. You bet I have got Mos now.

Friday, January 23, 1880

Once again evening comes and I have had one more day together with my Mosen. They go so fast that I am hardly aware of it before evening is at hand. Mos wanted to go to Clinton with letters for Marie today but we would not let him for it has not frozen yet and therefore the roads are wet and nasty. But this evening it looks like it will freeze. It is clear and lovely. The frost has already covered the bushes. Tomorrow we are expecting a lovely sight. I have been crocheting my curtain. Mother has now inspected it, and the M. on it means Mos of course, and if I can get another M on it, then it will be "my Mos." Tomorrow there will be a sermon in Liberty church and Sævig will preach. Excuse me, I was thinking that it was Saturday evening that I was writing this. Excuse me, my dear book. Now Mos is sitting and talking with Father and Mother. I will go to bed, my Mos.

Saturday, January 24, 1880

I got Father to give us permission to take Flora and the cutter. Now Mos is getting it ready. My dear little Mos and I, we are going to Cambridge, we are! I love little Mosen mine so much and am so happy that Mos could be with me during these days.

Bye-bye my book, I want to see if he is ready my own dear Mos. Evening. Another lovely day with my Mosen. We drove along over to Cambridge but when we got up to Vehus's road there was so much snow that we did not see a big log in the road. We drove into it and———tipped out, Mos and I, our clothing, the eggs, and the whole kit and kaboodle. Nothing was broken. We packed ourselves in and drove off again. I bought some dress material for Marie and myself. "Gray Mohair." When we got back we got dinner at Lars'. This evening I have made a bookmark for Marie, and Mos has helped me. Now Mos has gone to bed and I can hear him coughing up there. Doodneth, Mot, do you suppose I can sit here and write much now? No Mosi.

Excerpts from Ole's 1883 diary:

Monday, January 1, 1883

My Mosen gave me this book. Dear Mosen I love you so much. Happy New Year! God bless and protect my Mosen in this year. I drove to Stony Run, where there were church services, then drove home again right away. When I got home, O. Aslakson was here. He will stay here tonight. We have sat and talked together. He is an experienced man and it is fun and informative to talk with him.

Tuesday, January 2, 1883

Today in the morning Andrew and I went each in different directions and invited people to our party. We invited everyone in the congregation and some others. No schoolteacher came on the train. This evening the people came. They got supper, beer and wine, popcorn, apples, and cake and cigars. They amused themselves as best they could. Some of us sang. Two or three are now playing chess. And then they had other games. It is 12:30.

Wednesday, January 3, 1883, Friday evening

O. Aslakson and I drove out to Knut's to the teacher's meeting. Only Nupen was there. Still we had the meeting. I was made chairman, Knut, secretary. We carried on at Knut's and talked about putting together a school journal. In the evening Aslakson and I went over to Rollefson, where we stayed the night.[33]

Thursday, January 4, 1883

Knut and Nupen came over to Rollefson and we continued there. Rollefson was accepted as a member of the meeting. We discussed the inner coherence of the Catechism. Knut is intelligent, and Aslakson said about him that he has the makings of a capable educator.

Friday, January 5, 1883

Public meeting. We talked about the necessity of a school, about what kind of man would be suitable to run the school we need, and next about a seminary for schoolteachers. There was disagreement about the seminary. In the evening we drove home. There was to be a meeting at church in the evening, but not more than 5 came, even so Aslakson talked about the seminary. Dear Bissen has been at home alone. I love my Bis-Billebis.

Saturday, January 6, 1883

Read with the confirmands today. . . . At dinnertime it began to snow, and later it started to blow, so I did not go to Lisbon, but will wait until tomorrow. Bis and I have had a little clash today over several days' trouble, and now it is so good. I cannot be happy when there is a cloud in the skies of our love.

Wednesday, January 10, 1883

Cold today. Jørgen Lien went home. J. S. Johnson was here and paid me $161.50 pastor's wages. Then I went to Pillsbury and gave him $150. Money doesn't stay with me very long these days. Aslakson came back from Thorstenson, he is here now. We were out at Mrs. Hazelberg's for supper. We have talked a bit about "predestination."

Here is Ellen's diary from the same dates in 1883:

Monday, January 1, 1883

Happy New Year my book. I wonder what we will tell each other throughout this year? Let us begin and end in Jesus's name, and then all is well. Lina has helped me a little this afternoon. Mosen has been in Stony Run. This afternoon I had to bake for tomorrow evening, otherwise I will not be ready. Aslakson came this afternoon.

Tuesday, January 2, 1883

Was too sleepy to write this evening. We had our party. Andrew and Mosen went around and invited people. Everyone came except Mrs. Digen and Liberg. Lina helped me a little during the day too. Everything went well. The girls helped me with the table. There were about 46 here. We had popcorn, beer and apples to send around afterward.

Wednesday, January 3, 1883

It was hard to get up early today, but Mosen and Aslakson were to go to Stony Run. Well, it didn't get to be so early after all. I have cleaned up everywhere but not washed the floors. Will wash clothes tomorrow. No schoolteacher came here yesterday. Today a card came from one that it was too cold. Poor little ones. A whole package of "bier" came this evening.

Thursday, January 4, 1883

Mosen is still gone. I don't like to be here at home with Andrew, I get so tired of it. I have done a big washing today and scoured the floor. I am tired this evening. If only Mosen were at home. I was up to Neste this afternoon with a little popcorn for the children.

Friday, January 5, 1883

I don't like myself. A heavy and dark day.

Saturday, January 6, 1883

Mosen stayed at home this evening for it got to be such bad weather. Otherwise I would not have gotten to keep him here. This has been such a bad time. Now Bissen and I have spoken together and now we are Bislers again. Oh how I love my Mos. It has not been as good for a long time as it has been this evening. I had toothache all day.

Sunday, January 7, 1883

Bissus mine went to Lisbon this morning. It is so cold. My poor Bissus. I long so for my Mosen. I love him so much. Why am I not kind to Mosen. Just because I am bad! Mary Johnson came home with me from Sunday school. It is so cold to sleep alone. Many sweet goodnights Mosen from your Bissus.

Monday, January 8, 1883

My Bissus came home this evening. It is so good when Bissus comes. Poor Bissusen has frozen his nose when he was traveling west. I have washed today. Got a letter from home. They are so happy about their Christmas presents. . . . Dear Bissus is sleepy.

Tuesday, January 9, 1883

It snowed terribly today and later it became mild. This evening it has been terribly windy. Ole Vahl came with our lounge today. . . . Bissusen is scampy.

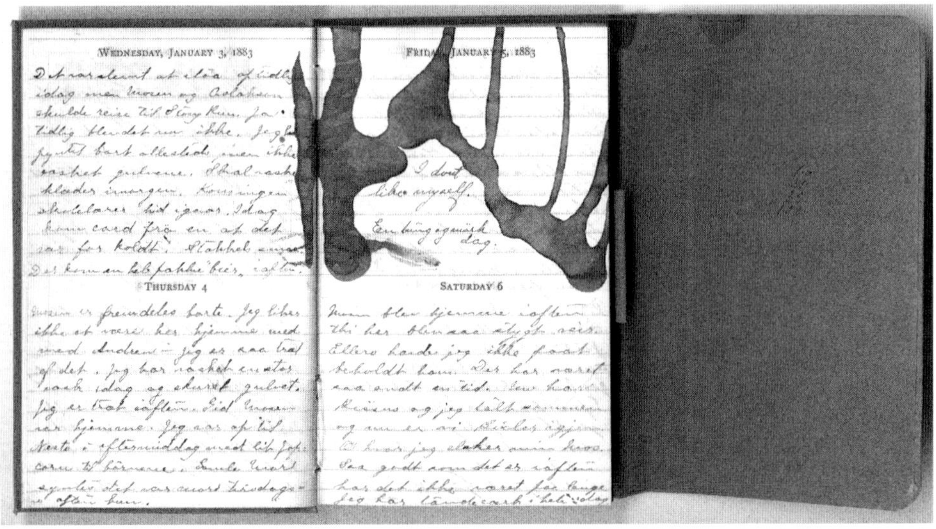

Figure 4. Ink spilled on the page of Ellen's diary entry for Friday, January 5, 1883, a day she calls a "heavy and dark day." Courtesy of the Norwegian American Historical Association, Northfield, Minnesota.

Wednesday, January 10, 1883

Today J. S. Johnson came with the pastor's salary. Mosen paid Pilsbyry $150.[34] It is cold today. Aslakson came back from Thorstenson and is here this evening. I have been knitting.

Thursday, January 11, 1883

Aslakson left today. Mosen has been at home. I have started to piece on a quilt. I am so tired this evening, yesterday evening we did not go to bed before 1 o'clock.

Now we return to Ole's diaries, this one from 1887. Their first-born child, a son Olaf, died at Easter time in 1885. Their second child, now seven months old and also named Olaf, has many nicknames. Most often they refer to him as "Tubbi."

Saturday, April 9, 1887, Easter Eve

Today 8 years ago Bis and I became engaged. Much has happened since then, but how good God has made everything for us! Thanks for His goodness and mercy! May He continue to accompany us, and lead us according to His will, and make us into His instruments, to Him the honor, to us the benefit. I read with the confirmands in the church in the forenoon. They have gotten water in the well now so they will stop digging, today they started to lay a frame over it. It has been windy today.

Sunday, April 10, 1887

There has not been much writing this week. Sunday was Easter. Tubbie went with us to church, but Mama had to go out with him again, he was frightened when I began to chant the liturgy. We did not have Sunday school. At 3 o'clock I drove to Montevideo. . . . In the evening it started to rain a little bit. During the church services it rained and there was lightning, but it stopped when we were going home, though it was very dark.

Monday, April 11, 1887

It had rained hard during the night. I was at the P. O., at Tvedt's, where I wrote a power of attorney for old Mrs. Tvedt, at Heiberg's, then I drove to Blom's and got a bottle of throat medicine from Mrs. Erik Halvorson, then off to Stony Run. On the way I met John Kittilson who drove with me to the church. It rained in the forenoon. After the church services I went to Samson and stayed there all day and all evening, and for the night too.

Tuesday, April 12, 1887

I read with the confirmands. When I was through, I drove to Tjødsvold's, his wife has been very sick, but was better now, then I drove home, where I arrived so early that I was able to order bran at the mill and wash the buggy before it got dark. In the evening we sang a little. Afterward I went down and listened to the debate between Y. Men's Club and our team. Resolved that

R.R. are more beneficial to the U.S. than navigation. Ours had the affirm. Ours won.

Wednesday, April 13, 1887

Our people were well satisfied with the outcome of the debate. There we can see the usefulness of debating in English as well. They could not have done this if we had not carried on with it this winter. They managed very well.—It rained during the night. In the evening I started to write my English sermon, which has been set for Sunday evening.

Thursday, April 14, 1887

I woke up when the doorbell rang, when I got up I found K. O. Neste, he asked me to come and baptize his little child, who was a few weeks old, it had become sick. I went and baptized it. In the middle of the rain, Mr. Day came with a load of hay for me. I took it, it is uncertain when we can get hay again. Frimanden was here and repaired the cistern pump.

Friday, April 15, 1887

Yesterday and today I have been working on my English sermon, I am almost finished now. Ladies Aid today . . . While I was there, Gustav Olson came, a Swede from the east side, and asked me to come and baptize his sick child. I went and baptized it. It had diphtheria, he said. Then I went home again. We got a letter from Marie and Kasberg, they got engaged on Easter eve. How wonderfully everything goes in this world!

Saturday, April 16, 1887

Saturday morning Mr. Captain Jacobson came, who has traveled on the oceans for 44 years and now lives in LaCrosse, but travels around and shows Bible pictures. . . . He stayed here during the day and the night. I read with the confirmands. . . . Nice weather.

Sunday, April 17, 1887

Sunday morning Jacobson and I drove to Rognestad's. First there were church services with communion in the schoolhouse, after that, I announced that Jacobson would give a show in the evening in the schoolhouse. We got dinner at Rognestad's, after that we drove home. In the evening I gave my English sermon. Luce and Bumpers were present as well as some other Americans.

Wednesday, April 27, 1887

Sunday evening. I don't write much in my book. Wednesday I was at home and worked around here a little, read a little, etc. There is so much to fix up in the spring both outside and in. In the evening we sang in church, there were not many, but it went well. Got a card that Engebret Braaten is dead.

Thursday, April 28, 1887

It was blowing terribly from the Northwest, and it was thick with dust up on the heights. I worked a little on the fence outside here, and with the stumps on the east side. While I was busy with that, a brother of tailor Bakken came and asked if I could come out to the funeral for Engebret Braaten. I took a book back to the library again. There will not be much reading now.

Friday, April 29, 1887

Nils Hanson Grande came and started to haul away the dirt from the banking around the house. I drove north to Braaten's. There was a strong wind. I drove the wrong way a little, for there have been big changes in just a few years. There were many people there. I spoke a little Norwegian and a little English in the house. From there they took the body to the Palmer Creek congregation's graveyard. After that I came home.

Sunday, May 1, 1887

92 degrees in the shade this morning. Had church services in the forenoon with communion, after that Sunday school. At 3:30 Bible class, and in the evening church services again. I did not use my clerical gown this evening, it is so much better, especially in the evening, when it is so hot, to not have to wear that heavy robe and the tight collar. It rained a little at 5 o'clock. Lien and Karl drove with Tillie and their horse.

Monday, May 2, 1887

Monday I drove out to Stony Run to a congregational meeting. Knut was elected as representative to the Synod meeting in Stoughton in June.

Tuesday, May 3, 1887

I went with Axel Jacobson to his school and stayed there until 10 o'clock, he is holding a Norwegian school. From there I drove to the church and read with the confirmands. In the evening Bis and I went to the hall and listened to Mrs. Muus's concert.[35] She had 3 boys and 1 girl with her, and they were good, though I didn't like the woman singer, but Olaf Moen, the 1st violinist, was excellent. There were many present.

Wednesday, May 4, 1887

Rasmus Knutson and wife, and Axel Jacobson were at the concert on Tuesday evening, and stayed overnight with us, they left early Wednesday morning. Anton Rystad came and talked about getting married in May, and then he brought his fiancée here, it is Marit Foss, she is going to stay here for a few days. Hartwick gave me free tickets to the concert. Mrs. Muus also gave a concert that evening, I was there, but not Bis.

Thursday, May 5, 1887

I spoke with Mrs. Muus on Wednesday evening after the concert. Thursday I met her at the hotel and she came with me up to our place and sat for a while. Marit Hamre had stayed here for the night. She left on the train to Minneapolis. Mrs. Muus went to Montevideo, where there was to be a concert in the evening. We had a congregational meeting in the evening and discussed whether Vikens should be accepted, talked about the graveyard, washing the church, evening church services, teachers' salaries to Decorah.

Friday, May 6, 1887

Before I was up today Connor came with a load of wood. He hauled my wood down from Weflen. Then Silverude came from Montevideo, he wanted to show me his stallions. Then Ekle's agent came from Mankato and I ordered a monument from him for $35. Then I got 32 bu. of oats which A. Vinsen sold me. After dinner Ingeborg and Lena Tjødsvold were here. I took the mares out to the horses, but they were not willing. This evening we sang, started in Song King.

Saturday, May 7, 1887

Crab blossoms. . . . Saturday it was hot and windy. I read with the confirmands. Started on the English explanation, it depends now on how it goes. Afternoon I drove to Stony Run and had communion registration. Afterward I went to Samson's and stayed there for the night. There is much dissatisfaction with the last congregational meeting.

Sunday, May 8, 1887

It was still very hot, but not so windy. There were 83 at communion, and 3 baptisms. . . . In the evening there were church services with communion in Montevideo. I was so tired in the evening. I stayed with G. Eliason for the night.

Wednesday, May 11, 1887

Today it has been a little fresher weather, but no rain came. I started to work on my English sermon for Sunday evening. In "Norden" it says that Dr. Walther in St. Louis died last week, 76 years old. We sang this evening, it went well, but there are so few basses again now.

Thursday, May 12, 1887

Thursday afternoon Bis and Tubbie and I took the train to Montevideo. G. Eliason met us at the depot with horse and buggy and we drove up to his place, from there to Tvedt's to Ladies Aid. Tvedts are going to go to Duluth soon. The husband has already left. During the night we stayed at Eliason's. In the evening the choir sang in church.

Sunday, May 15, 1887

Church services with communion in the forenoon. Then Sunday school. At 4 o'clock Bible class and in the evening English sermon. There were many Americans present. Weflen said there were more Americans than Norwegians. If only I were not so dependent on the manuscript. Tubbie was in church in the forenoon. Yesterday Miss Foss went home, is going to have her wedding on 2nd day of Pentecost.

Monday, May 16, 1887

Monday it was chillier. Afternoon Bis and I were up in the graveyard and put sod on Tubbie's grave.[36] I was so tired from hauling dirt and sod, but the grave was nice. It was really chilly, I thought. I had gotten a cold on the way home, so that in the evening I was not well at all. When I went to bed I got Wittenberg drops from Bissen.

Tuesday, May 17, 1887

Thronden was here for a while this afternoon. Bis and I went down to the hall, which was to be fixed up for the Ladies Aid sociable. It was held in the evening, it went well. At the auction and the collection for supper they took in over 52 doll. It will go to the church bells. There were many Americans. G. Johnson was the auctioneer.[37]

The following are excerpts from Ellen's spring 1887 diary:

Saturday, April 9, 1887

It has been so terribly hot today and this afternoon there was a little rain, not much, but it was very windy. The well diggers have come to a water vein. They have blasted the whole way. Today it is 8 years since our engagement day. That is to say, after Easter eve. Mosen gave me a lovely book "Maidenhood and Motherhood." These 8 years have gone quickly.

Sunday, April 10, 1887

Easter morning 2 years ago was a very terrible day. Then our sweet little friend wandered away. Now we have a little Tubbi again. Oh how God is good! Mosen is in Montevideo this evening.

Friday, April 15, 1887

Have been at Ladies Aid. . . . Tubbi was at home with Emily. When I came home there was a letter from Marie and Kasberg. They got engaged on Easter eve. God bless them and make them happy.

Saturday, April 16, 1887

Tubbi is 7 months old. An old man came today, who is named Jacobson. He shows pictures of the Bible with a Magic Lantern. Has many recommendations from pastors. I have finished my blue wrap today. Have also done a lot on the plaid polonaise. Got samples from O'Neil and Goodfellow and Co. Ole Axness is here too. Came from Montevideo this afternoon. Jacobsen is here too.

Sunday, April 17, 1887

Jacobson went with Mosen to Palmer Creek. Show there this evening. Mosen came back. Nice weather. I was out and drove with Tubbi for the first time in this buggy.

Monday, April 18, 1887

Mosen was in Stony Run. . . . Sent for some things today. This evening Jacobsen had a show in the church here. Were not many but it was very good.

Tuesday, April 19, 1887

Had to talk to Carl before I could get him to leave. Lazy good-for-nothing. We have so many here anyway now that there is the Teacher's Institute. He left then with his things and is going to leave early tomorrow for St. Paul.

Wednesday, April 27, 1887

I see in "Norden" that there has been a terrible tornado in Kansas. Have finished my dress. Have cut out nightgowns for Tubbi.

Thursday, April 28, 1887

Christine has helped us to sew today. It has been terribly windy. Tubbi is so good and so much fun, he comes up with so much.

Friday, April 29, 1887

Ladies Aid at Weflen's. We decided to have a sociable on the 17th of May in the Hall. Tubbi was at home with Emily.

Sunday, May 1, 1887

Today I went to communion. God help me and strengthen me, I am so often lukewarm and cold. This evening I have written home. Early today . . . Mrs. Townly got a daughter.

Monday, May 2, 1887

Cold rainy weather. Mosen went to Stony Run and has not come back again this evening. Has rained a little all day. I sent the silk to Marie.

Tuesday, May 3, 1887

Mosen came home this evening. Mrs. Martha Torkelson was here. I was up to Townly's and in town. Mosen and I were at the concert this evening. "Mrs. Muus Concert Co."

Wednesday, May 4, 1887

Anton Rexstad came with his girl and asked if she could get stand-by. We got free tickets. Marit Hamre got hers. Emily got from Miss Foss. They went this evening.

Thursday, May 5, 1887

Marit Hamre left today to her brother in Dak. Mrs. Muus was up here to us. She said it was the first time she had been in the home of a Synod pastor since she had left Goodhue.[38]

Friday, May 6, 1887

We are really puzzling over our dresses. I have started on my silk dress and Miss Foss on a brown silk, which is a wedding dress.

Mrs. Ireland is sewing it. We ordered a stone for little Olaf's grave today.

Monday, May 9, 1887

Emily washed and Margit helped her. Tubbi wants us to hold him almost all the time now. When Papa comes home he is so happy he trembles.

Tuesday, May 10, 1887

I have gotten to sew a little today, but have not finished it. Mrs. Hazelberg has finished pillow shams. We were in town this evening. Emily bought herself a white dress.

Wednesday, May 11, 1887

Got my dress almost finished. Emily has helped me to sew a lot today and Miss Foss helped me some too. Tubbi has been good.

Thursday, May 12, 1887

This afternoon we went to Montevideo. It was so hot and dusty. Tubbi was not afraid. Eliason met us with horse and buggy. Later drove to Ladies Aid at Tvedt's.

Friday, May 13, 1887

I went to town with Mrs. Halvorson and later Mrs. Eliason and I were over to Mrs. Lund. Eliason drove us to the depot again. In the meantime a hard rain shower came. When we got home Tubbi was happy. We went to Ladies Aid . . . and decided to have a sociable on the 17th of May. Today Miss Foss went home. She had finally finished her dress. I have set out my plants today. The air outside is fresh. Halvor Berg and wife were here. A man and wife came and asked for old clothes. Tubbi has been outside with me.

Sunday, May 15, 1887

I was in church with Tubbi. He was very good. This evening Mosen had English church services. I was at home with Stubbi.

Monday, May 16, 1887

Tubbi is 8 months, weighs 17 pounds. Emily ironed and I sewed a little. This afternoon we were up and fixed a little on Olaf's grave. It was so cold.

Tuesday, May 17, 1887

We baked in the forenoon. In the afternoon I was at the hall and fixed things. This evening we had our sociable. It went extra well, took in over $50.

Solveig Zempel *is St. Olaf professor emerita of Norwegian. She taught Norwegian language and literature, served as associate dean, and held the Boldt Distinguished Chair in the Humanities. She has published translations of Norwegian-American letters, as well as several works by O. E. Rölvaag. She has also served on the NAHA board.*

NOTES

1. Portions of this article have been presented at various academic conferences and published in conference proceedings, including "'My Book, I Have Neglected You Sorely': Reading the Kravik-Lokensgaard Diaries," *Swedish-American Historical Quarterly* 56, nos. 2–3 (April–July 2005): 198–208.
2. See Jennifer Sinor, *The Extraordinary Work of Ordinary Writing: Annie Ray's Diary* (Iowa City: University of Iowa Press, 2002), 17.
3. Elizabeth Hampsten, *Read This Only to Yourself: The Private Writings of Midwestern Women 1880–1910* (Bloomington: Indiana University Press, 1982), 14, 15.
4. Much of the background information on Ellen and Ole has been supplied by their grandson David Hardy and is found in publications prepared for the family. Copies of these privately printed materials are available in the archives of the Norwegian American Historical Association, Northfield, Minnesota.
5. For the sake of consistency, the spelling "Lokensgard" used by the American family is the one used throughout this article.
6. There are a number of excellent histories of Norwegian migration to America. See, for example, Theodore C. Blegen, *Norwegian Migration to America*, vols. 1 and 2 (Northfield, MN: Norwegian American Historical Association, 1931, 1940); Odd S. Lovoll, *The Promise of America: A History of the Norwegian-American People* (Minneapolis: University of

Minnesota Press, 1984); Hans Norman and Harald Runblom, *Transatlantic Connections: Nordic Migration to the New World after 1800* (Oslo: Norwegian University Press, 1987); Ingrid Semmingsen, *Norway to America: A History of the Migration* (Minneapolis: University of Minnesota Press, 1978).

7. David V. Mollenhoff, *Madison: A History of the Formative Years* (Dubuque, IA: Kendall/Hunt, 1982), 145, 151.
8. Steven Stowe, "Making Sense of Letters and Diaries," History Matters: The U.S. Survey on the Web, July 2002, http://historymatters.gmu.edu.
9. This topic has been studied by, for example, Molly McCarthy, "A Pocketful of Days: Pocket Diaries and Daily Record Keeping among Nineteenth-Century New England Women," *New England Quarterly* 73, no. 2 (June 2000): 274–96. Her article does not mention that diaries might have been kept in languages other than English.
10. Orm Øverland, "Learning to Read Immigrant Letters: Reflections towards a Textual Theory," in *Norwegian-American Essays 1996* (Oslo: NAHA-Norway, Norwegian Emigrant Museum, 1996), 213–14.
11. Øverland, "Learning to Read Immigrant Letters," 220.
12. Kristofer Janson was a Norwegian poet, author, and Unitarian minister who lived for a time in the United States. See Nina Draxten, *Kristofer Janson in America* (Boston: Published for the Norwegian American Historical Association by Twayne Publishers, 1976).
13. Both Ellen and Ole used many nicknames for each other, including *Mosen, Mosa, Bis, Bissen,* etc.
14. J. C. Dundas was a well-known Norwegian-American physician.
15. Bjørnstjerne Bjørnson, a famous Norwegian writer, was on a speaking tour of the Midwest. See Eva Haugen, *Home of the Free: Bjørnstjerne Bjørnson's American Letters of 1880–1881* (Northfield, MN: Norwegian American Historical Association, 1978).
16. Hogan quoted in Suzanne L. Bunkers and Cynthia A. Huff, *Inscribing the Daily: Critical Essays on Women's Diaries* (Amherst: University of Massachusetts Press, 1996), 5.
17. Robert A. Fothergill, *Private Chronicles: A Study of English Diaries* (London: Oxford University Press, 1974), 9.
18. *Bis* is one of Ole's many nicknames for Ellen.
19. Stowe, "Making Sense of Letters and Diaries."
20. David Fitzpatrick, *Oceans of Consolation: Personal Accounts of Irish Migration to Australia* (Ithaca, N.Y.: Cornell University Press, 1994).
21. Sinor, *Extraordinary Work of Ordinary Writing,* 28.
22. Laurel Thatcher Ulrich, *A Midwife's Tale: The Life of Martha Ballard, Based on Her Diary, 1785–1812* (New York: Alfred A. Knopf, 1991), 9.
23. Stowe, "Making Sense of Letters and Diaries."
24. Lynn Bloom, quoted in Cynthia A. Huff, "Reading as Re-vision: Approaches to Reading Manuscript Diaries," *Biography* 23, no. 3 (Summer 2000): 509.
25. Marilyn Ferris Motz, "The Private Alibi: Literacy and Community in the Diaries of Two Nineteenth-Century American Women," in Bunkers and Huff, *Inscribing the Daily,* 191.
26. Arthur Ponsonby, a cataloger of English diaries, as quoted in Thomas Mallon, *A Book of One's Own: People and Their Diaries* (New York: Ticknor and Fields, 1984), xvi–xvii.
27. Anthony Quinn, "Dear Diary: How Keeping a Journal Can Bring You Daily Peace," *Guardian,* August 21, 2021, https://www.theguardian.com/lifeandstyle/2021/aug/21/dear-diary-how-keeping-a-journal-can-bring-you-daily-peace.

28. Pastor Bernt Julius Muus was a prominent Norwegian-American clergyman and is mentioned frequently in the diaries. He was sued by his wife to recover her inheritance from her father and later to gain a legal separation. This created considerable scandal among Norwegian-Americana Lutherans.
29. Norway's Constitution Day was often celebrated by Norwegian Americans.
30. Here Ellen writes in Ole's diary. The rest of this entry is in her hand.
31. "The Church Times," a church periodical.
32. In January 1880, Prof. F. A. Schmidt put out the first of a number of publications entitled *Altes und Neues* [Old and new].
33. Ole has handwritten "Friday evening" here to indicate that he wrote the entry on a different day than was printed on the page.
34. Ellen's spelling of *Pillsbury.*
35. Information on Pastor B. J. Muus and Mrs. Muus can be found in Joseph Shaw, *Bernt Julius Muus: Founder of St. Olaf College* (Northfield, MN: Norwegian American Historical Association, 1999) and Kathryn Ericson, "Triple Jeopardy: The Muus vs. Muus case in Three Forums," *Minnesota History* 50, no. 8 (1987): 298–308.
36. Their first son, Olaf Herman, nicknamed Tubbie, died on Easter morning 1885. Their second son was also named Olaf Herman and also nicknamed Tubbie.
37. The last entry in Ole's 1887 diary is 30 May. The rest is blank except for a few notes and cash accounts at the end.
38. Mrs. Muus was granted legal separation from Pastor B. J. Muus, an important churchman mentioned frequently in these diaries.

Creating a Sense of Place

NORWEGIAN ETHNICIZATION IN THE PACIFIC NORTHWEST, 1870–1960

Terje Mikael Hasle Joranger

With a view toward the majestic Olympic Mountains, the city of Poulsbo is situated along the bottom of Liberty Bay on a peninsula between Puget Sound and Hood Canal in the northern part of Kitsap County.[1] With a population of about 13,000 inhabitants, the city has been defined as a Norwegian town for more than a century due to the significant presence of a Norwegian-American population and the parading of Norwegian-American ethnicity.[2] One hundred and seventy miles south of Poulsbo we find Puget Island, a flat and oblong island located within the boundary of Wahkiakum County on the Washington side of the Columbia River. Poulsbo and Puget Island, both located in the Pacific Northwest, were settled by Norwegian immigrants in the last decades of the nineteenth century and are two out of a number of ethnic communities in the region. The Pacific Northwest is an understudied region in Norwegian-American historiography and deserves more scholarly attention.[3] In this article, I will focus on the symbols and myths used among Norwegian immigrants in Poulsbo and Puget Island, which were part of a negotiation and ethnicization process from the period of settlement (1870–1900) until 1960.

The processes of translocal transplantation and spatial orientation in the Norwegian communities of Poulsbo and Puget Island were created in an American environment in the Pacific Northwest. They are similar to a number of Norwegian ethnic communities that were created in the Upper Midwest, but they differ both in the timing of their establishment and in their spatial orientation. Despite their differences, the creation of symbolic ties between sending regions in Norway and receiving regions both in the Northwest Pacific and in the Upper Midwest have in common that they may be regarded as a part of the negotiation process. This process takes place between inhabitants of Norwegian origin and an American environment in order to establish a sense of place in American society where Norwegian Americans could enjoy the benefits of being both Norwegian and American.

The Norwegians and other settlers created new societies on lands that had been inhabited by many Native American nations for centuries. The settler societies brought a different understanding of the use of the land than that of the

Figure 1. Puget Island from Cathlamet, Washington, toward the north. It is linked to the mainland by the Julia Butler Hansen Bridge. Photograph by Pete Forsyth licensed under the Creative Commons Attribution 3.0 Unported license. Courtesy of Wikimedia Commons, https://commons.wikimedia.org/wiki/File:Puget_Island_from_the_north.jpg.

Indigenous populations. The latter typically regarded land as a common resource, and they often lived with the land more closely in alignment with the modern concept of sustainability. Settler populations, however, brought with them new values: they embraced private ownership of land and regarded land as a commodity. European and American expeditions to the Pacific Northwest in the late eighteenth and early nineteenth centuries brought the attention of the federal authorities.[4] In 1785, the Continental Congress passed the Northwest Ordinance, which prescribed the survey of the land and the subsequent sale of parcels of land for centuries to come.[5] Various Native nations relinquished (through force, trickery, or otherwise) their rights to the lands to federal authorities throughout the nineteenth century. The westward movement of settlers transformed the landscape along the way.[6] Members of the Suquamish nation, for example, lived in portions of the Puget Sound region, including what we now call Island, San Juan, and Kitsap Counties on the east side of Puget Sound. In 1855, Washington Territory's new governor and the commissioner of Indian affairs met with the Suquamish in order to negotiate an agreement to make it lawful for loggers and settlers to move onto the ancestral land of the Suquamish. In the Treaty of Point Elliott, the Suquamish ceded their rights in seven counties. In return, the Indigenous population was to be protected from the intrusion of the settlers, but only on their allotted land at the Port Madison Indian Reservation.[7] The Clatsop and Kathlamet nations were also living in the Puget Sound region prior of the coming of the settlers. Many important place-names in the Pacific Northwest originate from Indigenous languages.[8]

Founding Two Norwegian Enclaves in Washington State

In his book *West of the Great Divide,* Kenneth O. Bjork convincingly writes that favorable reports in Norwegian-language newspapers in the Midwest created an awareness of nature and resources in the Pacific Northwest.[9] According to Bjork, three main factors explain the big influx of Scandinavians to the Pacific Northwest in the last decades of the nineteenth century: the "openness" of the region with large and varied stretches of free or cheap land, its large opportunities for investment, and the future for speculators who regarded the territory's "resources of soil, forest, mines, and waters as well as in its strategic location for east-west trade."[10] In 1883, the Northern Pacific Railway finished its line to Portland. Ten years later the Great Northern Railway established their terminus in Seattle, while a third line, the Chicago, Milwaukee, & St. Paul, reached Tacoma in 1909. The railroads created efficient and direct links between the Midwest and the Pacific Northwest. Their quick and effective access to the Pacific Northwest resulted not only in a mass influx of settlers but also in the transfer of money, information, skills, and technical knowledge from areas farther east, which in turn initiated a boom period for the region.[11]

In many letters and a series of articles, reporters for the Norwegian-language newspapers stressed the need for attracting more Norwegians to the Pacific Northwest region. Norwegian settlement in Washington Territory (which would become Washington state in 1889) in many ways was a continuation of a homogeneous settlement pattern in the Midwest, replicating place-names and regional settlement patterns.[12]

Jorgen Martinus Eliason is credited with being the first white person to settle on the present site of Poulsbo, then Washington Territory, joining a single Norwegian settler who settled on the bay seven years earlier. Jorgen Eliason immigrated to America as a young man and for a time lived in White-hall, Michigan, but he traveled as a widower to Seattle with his six-year-old son in 1881. He was later joined by his sister, and the three settled on a vacated logging camp on Dogfish Bay (present-day Liberty Bay) on the present site of Poulsbo two years later. The first settlers endured hardships due to isolation and the endless job of clearing the land to establish a home in the wilderness. Jorgen Eliason donated a portion of his land to the first Lutheran congregation in the area to form a church and a cemetery. The congregation was given the name Fordefjord Lutheran Church in Jorgen Eliason's honor, replicating similar naming patterns in the settlement process among Norwegians in the Midwest. Giving names in their own language created a sense of identity in new surroundings, and, as in this example, the name often reflected regional origins in Norway.[13]

Figure 2. Sunday School of Fordefjord Lutheran Church. Congregation Records. Courtesy of the Norwegian American Historical Association in Northfield, Minnesota.

Another transplanted name is evident in the example of Iver Brynildsen Moe, who arrived in present-day Poulsbo a few months after Jorgen Eliason with his wife, Anne Kirstina, and their three children. A native of Kornsjø in Idd parish near Halden in Østfold, Norway, Iver Moe operated a store at Paulsbomoen prior to his emigration to America with his family in 1880.[14] As Iver Moe gave land for the platting of a village in 1886, he was given the task to provide a name for the post office. He named the new post office on Dogfish Bay after Paulsbo, his last home in Norway. By naming Poulsbo (which was misspelled with an *o* instead of an *a* because the postal authorities in Washington, DC, had misinterpreted Moe's handwriting) after his old home in Norway, he not only created a personal link between his former and his new home but also established a symbolic ethnic denominator in an Anglo-American world.[15]

A steady influx of Norwegian settlers arrived in Poulsbo in the following years, influenced by Iver Moe's letters in Norwegian-language newspapers to an extent. In a letter printed in the newspaper *Norden* in 1887, Moe writes about the quick development of the village. He only found two houses in Poulsbo at the time of his arrival, he writes, one of them occupied by a Norwegian. By the time that he wrote the letter, Poulsbo had grown to be a substantial Norwegian settlement, including a post office, a schoolhouse, a congregation with a resident pastor, and a courthouse. Finally, Moe suggests that migration was based on similar work as in Norway: "We Norwegians are a coast people who are accustomed to the sea, fishing, and logging, and here are just the conditions that suit us."[16]

Several observers perceived the two communities settled by Norwegian immigrants as translocal and romantic transplantations from Northern Norway. Besides, they saw parallels between the character-building among the population who lived along the rugged coast of Norway and the hardships encountered by their descendants who immigrated to the Pacific Northwest. Observers also compared the struggle of immigrants in the Pacific Northwest to the land-taking process in the Icelandic Sagas.

Norwegian settlements around Poulsbo were based on immigration from specific regions in Norway, again replicating regional settlement patterns among Norwegians in the Midwest. For example, the Vinland settlement is located on the peninsula west of Poulsbo, Breidablik lies north, and Gudbrandsdalen northeast of Poulsbo. These locations, bearing Norwegian names, were primarily settled by Norwegians. Immigrants hailing from Heidal parish in the Gudbrandsdal region made up the majority in the Gudbrandsdalen settlement and formed the only direct migrant group in the Poulsbo area, arriving in 1890. Immigrants from Trøndelag and Northern Norway, especially from Mosjøen, Sandnessjøen, and Mo i Rana, were represented in Vinland, whereas Norwegians from the eastern and southern parts of Norway made up the majority in the Breidablik settlement. Two settlements, Scandia and Pearson, south and southeast of Poulsbo, were primarily settled by Swedes.[17]

Some Norwegians established a colony on Puget Island near the mouth of the Columbia River. Most were salmon fishers and worked as loggers, but many were young men who eventually became farmers after they had cut down the large trees on the island. The first Norwegian settlers arrived in the 1880s, attracted by rich salmon fisheries in the Columbia River, and in 1892 about forty individuals were living on the island.[18] Their reports to friends and relatives in Norway strengthened the presence of this regional group, and a Lutheran congregation was organized in 1893. So many of the island's population were Norwegian that the island received the name Little Norway.[19] The Norwegian immigrants, however, referred to it as "Øylandet," the Island Country. A majority of the population originated from the communities of Brønnøy, Sømna, and Vega in South Helgeland in Northern Norway, and Puget Island was supposedly the largest concentration of emigrants from South Helgeland in the United States.[20] Most settlers were working as lumbermen and fishermen, and they retained their cultural traits due to the relative isolation of the island. Many fishermen combined fishing in the Columbia River with fishing during summers in Alaska. The immigrants from the seaboard communities of Northern Norway were accustomed to winter fishing along the Lofoten Islands. As immigrants to the Pacific Northwest, they took part in the seasonal summer fisheries for halibut, herring, cod, and salmon in Alaska along with other fishermen from Cathlamet.[21] A Sons of Norway lodge and a local school were established in the early part of the twentieth century. The island was developed further with the building of dikes around the island in 1916–1917, thus eliminating the chance of flooding. This brought progress to Puget Island and facilitated the expansion of arable land in that several thousand acres of land were put under cultivation on the island.[22]

Scandinavians

Poulsbo and Puget Island represent two out of a large number of Norwegian ethnic enclaves in Washington. They are also representative of the areas with the highest concentration of Norwegians around 1900.[23] By 1890, Scandinavians made up 23.4 percent of all foreign-born people in the newly established Washington state. Surpassed by the Swedes, who made up 11.4 percent of the total number of foreign-born people that year, Norwegians made up 9.3 percent and Danes 3.1 percent of the total.[24] The concentration of Norwegians was part of a substantial influx of Scandinavian immigrants; between 1890 and 1910, more than 150,000 Scandinavians settled in the Pacific Northwest. The state of Washington received the majority of these immigrants, and by 1910, Scandinavians made up the largest ethnic group in the state. They constituted over 20 percent of the foreign-born population. Many newcomers from Norway, Sweden, and Denmark settled in Seattle and other cities in the Pacific Northwest. In 1940, almost 20,000 first-generation Scandinavian immigrants were living in Seattle, making up 30 percent of the foreign-born population.[25]

In his study *From All Points: America's Immigrant West, 1870s–1952,* Elliott Robert Barkan states that earlier studies take Scandinavians' assimilation for granted. Instead, in Scandinavian areas dominated by the logging business, in coastal shipping, and in the salmon and halibut industries Scandinavian men and women established a rich organizational life with homeland-rooted associations based on their national origins.[26] Scandinavians were culturally and racially regarded as white to Americans, which stood in stark contrast to the treatment of Mexican, Japanese, or Chinese immigrants and their descendants. According to Barkan, "the broad compatibility between Scandinavian and American cultural, religious, and even physical characteristics eased these newcomers' acceptance and accommodation to life in the Pacific Northwest."[27]

The relationship between Native Americans and the newcomers was entangled and not always good. Yet the newcomers praised the future prospects in the Pacific Northwest and were instrumental in attracting other Scandinavians, as well as other ethnic groups, to the region.[28] The distinctive ethnic settlement pattern among Scandinavian groups near Poulsbo resulted in the formation of separate organizations. For example, Swedish settlers from Lemolo and Pearson Point formed the Lucia Bride contest in 1907. Only many years later was the ceremony added to the Christmas activities among the Norwegians.[29] Scandinavians enjoyed more cooperation in economic life as both Norwegian and Swedish immigrants formed businesses in Poulsbo.[30] According to Dag Blanck, Norwegian–Swedish relations were characterized by separateness in the period between 1890 and World War I, breaking the earlier Pan-Scandinavian trend characterized by cooperation between the two groups. As a result, organizations and church bodies were developed along different ethnic lines.[31] Scandinavians in Poulsbo and on Puget Island were no exception. There is little evidence of

Figure 3. Ladies' Aid of Fordefjord Lutheran Church. Congregation Records. Courtesy of the Norwegian American Historical Association in Northfield, Minnesota.

cooperation in organizational and church life between Norwegians and Swedes during the time period studied here.[32] Norwegians made up the majority group, thereby representing what Kathleen Neils Conzen refers to as a "localization of culture." The dominant position of the Norwegians put their mark on the social and economic activities in Poulsbo, thereby branding it as an ethnic community and creating a sense of place from an early date.[33]

During a Norse declamatory contest for the Sigvald Quale Silver Medal in Poulsbo in 1940, Kristine Haugen shared her reflections about the settling of Poulsbo in *Decorah-Posten.* In a romantic tone she praised the settlers, the *Landnaamsmænd,* who found work as lumberjacks and in sawmills and who later cleared the land in order to establish their homes. Here she compared the settlers in Poulsbo with the Norse settlers who participated in the land-taking and colonization of Iceland as mentioned in the Icelandic Saga literature:

"Show me a place on Earth that reminds us more about the beautiful homeland from which the people had to part when they went on a journey to foreign lands," she wrote in romantic terms. She referred to a similar climate as in coastal areas in Norway and also praised the people of Poulsbo for keeping the Norwegian heritage alive.[34]

Ethnic Landscapes: Myths and Symbols

In articles a few years later, observers drew similar comparisons between the hardships of the settlers in America and their struggles at sea in Norway, as well as the similarities in landscapes. By then the United States had entered the Second World War, which eventually was to affect the two ethnic communities considerably. According to a sociology study made in 1960, Poulsbo saw a change in its orientation from logging, fishing, and farming to become an urban, industrialized community. At the beginning of World War Two, Poulsbo was characterized by close-knit relations between its inhabitants and a "high degree of ethnic unity" where individuals stressed independence and a sense of equality. After 1940, Poulsbo saw an increase in the number of businesses established by newcomers and the introduction of new ideas. The new men, who settled in Poulsbo because they liked it, became the boosters of the town through their involvement in public affairs. Thus, during the war, the isolated, small community increased more than threefold, overwhelming many members of the community.[35]

The parallels between the Poulsbo area and Norway as mentioned by observers reflect a sense of translocal identity-building as they indicate a comparison with the former and the present homes of the immigrants.[36] The references are mentioned in several articles. In "Vort Folk ved Havet" [Our people by the sea] in *Decorah-Posten,* for example, I. H. Myrvang focuses on the history of his home, the city of Svolvær in Northern Norway. He starts his articles by referring to the landscape around Seattle and Bremerton, consisting of "fjords and tall mountains" with settlements scattered along the many inlets and in the valleys. The author especially refers to his home church, the Vinland Lutheran Church. The population at this specific location is mixed, but everywhere their ancestral ties could be traced back both to the settlement areas farther east and, for many of them, to Northern Norway. This introduction leads us to the main story: namely, a personal journey to the city of Svolvær, including a presentation of its location among the Lofoten Islands and its history.[37]

Reflections on the ties between the landscapes of the Pacific Northwest and those of Northern Norway in times of war are also evident in two articles written by Norwegian-born Lise Lindbæk, who visited Puget Island in 1944. Lindbæk was the first Norwegian female correspondent of war and at the time had fled the war scene in Europe. Arriving in the United States, she acquired a temporary job with the Norwegian-language newspaper *Nordisk Tidende*. She went on a lecture

Figure 4. Vinland Scandinavian Evangelical Lutheran Church. Congregation Records. Courtesy of the Norwegian American Historical Association in Northfield, Minnesota.

tour around the country. It was during this tour that Lindbæk visited the Pacific Northwest and the state of Washington.[38] The visit to the island on the Columbia River on 9 April 1944 was symbolic, being the date of the German occupation of Norway four years earlier. As a majority of the population hailed from Northern Norway, this reminded her of a trip to the mining community of Sulitjelma in Nordland in Northern Norway in 1938. Lindbæk stressed the connections between the conditions in Sulitjelma and on Puget Island; while she deemed the surroundings on Puget Island as "less dramatic" than those in Northern Norway, "good work here has also overcome supposedly invincible natural difficulties; . . . here the same singing and soft Nordland dialect is spoken, a clean and hearty language." She concludes by stating that "this island has become a fairy tale of happiness and progress, due to the . . . courage, [and] invincible stubbornness . . . that has always characterized the people of Northern Norway at home and today more than ever."[39]

The articles have two implications. First, they bear reference to perceptions of a transplanted "New Northern Norway," where the observers create a translocal connection between the population in the Pacific Northwest and the region of origin of a large number of these immigrants. Second, the articles may also be regarded as a reaction to the waning ethnic flavor of the two communities as a consequence of the economic and social development that took place in the region after World War II. In 1953, Alfred Apsler, a journalist in the *Sunday Oregonian Magazine,* corroborates this view. Although "rudiments of the old country ways are still in evidence," he noted, "the idyll of the isolated Norwegian fishing village in the midst of a foreign continent is about ended" and "Puget Island is unalterably becoming a part of America." A bridge connecting Puget Island with the Cathlamet village on the north shore of the Columbia River was completed in 1939, and in 1953 the Puget Island school closed its doors and the classes were transferred to the new school in Cathlamet. Consequently, the relative isolation of the community was broken, and the economic life of the island lay open to influence from the outside world.[40] The post office and local stores on Puget Island also closed, and the inhabitants of Puget Island had to travel to Cathlamet to send their mail and buy their groceries. The difference may be attributed to a changing economic development in the region, including centralization, negative prospects in agriculture, and forest protection of large, forested areas. The changes had a significant impact on the Norwegians on Puget Island, and it became difficult for them to conduct their traditional way of life.[41]

Dual Landscapes

In his presidential address at the Organization of American Historians in Atlanta, Georgia, in 2014, Alan M. Kraut discussed the postmigration negotiation of identity in the United States. According to Kraut, assimilation, which is a much-contested term among historians, is tied to an "adaptation between native and newcomer, characterized by an ongoing negotiation that each newcomer conducts over the price of opportunity in the United States."[42] The source material describing the two Norwegian enclaves in the state of Washington indicates that its ethnicization developed through a process of negotiation over time. This negotiation has taken place among Norwegian Americans, between the ethnic group and other ethnic groups in the region, and also between the ethnic group and the greater society. Their attitude toward the surrounding landscapes may be referred to "ethnic landscapes," which indicates that ethnic groups create distinctive geographies in social, spatial, and symbolic terms.[43] The term is congruent with sociologist Anthony D. Smith's assertion that landscapes associated with an ancestral past would influence a national identity among migrant peoples. According to Smith, national identity and "national character" are more influenced by "collective perceptions encoded in myths and symbols, of the ethnic 'meanings' of particular stretches of territory, and the ways in which such stretches . . . are turned into 'homelands' inextricably tied to the 'fate' of their communities." Smith argues that "myths, memories, values and symbols" form the "core" of ethnicity.[44] In relevance to this study, the creation of a myth interlinking the settler hardships in the Pacific Northwest with the hardships encountered in a struggle for subsistence in a harsh climate in Norway strengthened an ethnic Norwegian identity in America. Besides, the comparisons made between Norwegian and Norwegian-American article writers between the fjords and mountains of the Norwegian home area of settlers with similar surroundings in the Pacific Northwest had the same purpose in a period of social unrest.[45] Despite the emphasis on Norwegian ties in the articles mentioned, the communities were neither Norwegian nor American in terms of social, economic, and cultural life but instead were Norwegian-American.

Over time, myths and symbols take the place of ethnic traits following the gradual disappearance of language, which is consistent with Barbro Klein's study on symbolism among Swedish Americans. She shows that symbolic markers such as artifacts, ethnic celebrations, and lutefisk suppers in Lutheran churches are ethnic in their content, referring to Swedish origins. However, the symbolism must be American in order to be accepted in society.[46] In this process, the creation of myths and symbols tied to transplanted place-names and the comparison between ethnic landscapes in the Pacific Northwest were a response to the integration of formerly homogeneous communities into the economy of the entire region.

Terje Mikael Hasle Joranger *is the research director at the Norwegian Emigrant Museum and professor in history at the Inland Norway University of Applied Sciences. He is professionally responsible for Crossings 200 in Norway and is the editor of* Norwegian-American Essays *(NAHA-Norge).*

NOTES

1. This article is a revised version of the author's presentation "Creating a Sense of Place: Norwegian Ethnicization in the Pacific Northwest, 1870–1900" held at the conference Nordic Immigration in the Pacific Northwest from Then to Now—Technology, Innovation, and Migration, hosted by the National Nordic Museum, Seattle, March 16, 2016.
2. Poulsbo, Washington, today has a population of 13,010. City of Poulsbo, "Velkommen til Poulsbo . . . Welcome!," accessed July 25, 2024, https://www.cityofpoulsbo.com/.
3. More recent secondary sources on the Pacific Northwest include Janet E. Rasmussen, *New Land, New Lives: Scandinavian Immigrants to the Pacific Northwest* (Northfield, MN: Norwegian American Historical Association; Seattle: University of Washington, 1993); Rita Johansen, *Norske øyværinger i Columbia River* [The story of Norwegian islanders in the Columbia River] (Mosjøen, Norway: Frifant Vega, 1999); Rangvald Kvelstad, ed., *Poulsbo: Its First Hundred Years* (Silverdale, WA: Silverdale Printer, 1986); Gordon Strand, *Voices of Ballard and Beyond: Stories of Immigrants and Their Descendants in the Pacific Northwest* (Seattle: Heritage Nordic Museum, 2012); Fred Poyner IV, *Pacific Fishermen, Inc.: 150 Years of Norwegian Heritage Shipbuilding* (Seattle: Classic Day Publishing, 2022); Fred Poyner IV, "Stories from Stanwood's

Waterfront and the Stillaguamish River Valley: A Collective Portrait of a Norwegian Pioneer Community," *Vesterheim* 20, no. 1 (2022): 4–10; Fred Poyner IV, *One Family, Two Continents: The Swasands and Aleutian Spray Fisheries, Inc.* (Honolulu: Legacy Isle Publishing, 2023). See also Elliott Robert Barkan, *From All Points: America's Immigrant West, 1870s–1952* (Bloomington: Indiana University Press, 2007).

4. Kvelstad, *Poulsbo,* 9–12.
5. Hildegard Binder Johnson, *Order upon the Land* (New York: Oxford University Press, 1976), 43–46.
6. See, for example, Ray Allen Billington, *Westward Expansion: A History of the American Frontier* (New York: Macmillan, 1960).
7. Kvelstad, *Poulsbo,* 13–23.
8. The city of Seattle was named after a leader of the Suquamish nation, Chief Seattle. Wahkiakum County, in which Puget Island is located, has its name from a Kathlamet nation village located on the north bank of the Columbia River near the present town of Cathlamet. *Wahkiakum* translates to "tall timber" in the Chinook language, while the name *Cathlamet* comes from the word *Calamet* in the same language, meaning "stone." The Kathlamet nation got its name due to the fact that they were living along a stretch of rocky riverbed. Wahkiakum County, "History of Wahkiakum County," https://www.co.wahkiakum.wa.us/389/Wahkiakum-County.
9. Kenneth O. Bjork, *West of the Great Divide: Norwegian Migration to the Pacific Coast, 1847–1893* (Northfield, MN: Norwegian American Historical Association, 1958), 300–03.
10. Bjork, *West of the Great Divide,* 431.
11. Odd S. Lovoll, *Norwegian Newspapers in America: Connecting Norway and the New Land* (St. Paul: Minnesota Historical Society Press, 2010), 183, 189; Bjork, *West of the Great Divide,* 450–54. The completion of the transcontinental railroad to the Pacific Northwest was the result of the rise of mass transfer in the wake of the Industrial Revolution in America in the early decades of the nineteenth century. The expansion on the American continent that followed not only included an Anglo-prone mass transfer of goods and people but also was matched by the transfer of money, information, skills, and technical knowledge. James Belich, *Replenishing the Earth: The Settler Revolution and the Rise of the Anglo World, 1783–1939* (Oxford: Oxford University Press, 2009), 106–44.
12. One correspondent in 1872 wrote: "Those with whom I talked felt well satisfied with their lot and greeted me with heartiness as they gave me slyly to understand that they wished I could, by mentioning them publicly, help them get their neighbors and good Christian wives from among people of their own nationality." *Fædrelandet og emigranten,* 25 May 1871, quoted in Bjork, *West of the Great Divide,* 304–6. In *Decorah-Posten* in 1887, Iver Moe responded to a reader of the newspaper from Lac qui Parle County, Minnesota, stating that "all of us who reside here have lived in Minnesota and Dakota or other states in the east, but," he added, "we chose to travel to Washington Territory" (my translation). He also asked individuals who wanted to settle in the area to write to him in person, as he wanted to respond all letters in a thorough manner. Letter in *Decorah-Posten,* November 9, 1887.
13. Personal contacts seem to explain his choice of location. Seven years earlier, Ole Stubbhaug of Naustdal in Sunnfjord, Norway, was the first Norwegian to settle on the bay, and there were kinship ties between his wife's family and those of Jorgen's deceased wife. Kvelstad, *Poulsbo,* 31–34, 38–39.

14. The family first settled in Minneapolis but took up a homestead in the Red River Valley the following year. After the family had hired out to work on the Northern Pacific Railroad in Montana, they arrived in Seattle in 1883 and eventually landed on Dogfish Bay. A. B. Moe, *Journey to Seattle and Pioneering at Puget Sound,* n.d., Box 1523, Local History Washington, Norwegian American Historical Association.
15. Kvelstad, *Poulsbo,* 39, 52; Jens Bakke, "Poulsbo: Historien om utvandreren Iver B. Moe," *Ida* (2001): 87. His last name was derived from *Paulsbomoen,* the location where Iver Moe ran a store prior to emigration.
16. Letter in *Norden,* 31 May 1887; Bjork, *West of the Great Divide,* 434, 442, 445–46. Ole Stubb from Førde in Sunnfjord, Norway, is credited with being the first settler on Dogfish Bay, arriving here from Michigan in 1876. Jorgen Eliason, also from Førde in Sunnfjord, arrived with his family to Dogfish Bay the same year as Iver Moe. Kvelstad, *Poulsbo,* 32–33, 38–43.
17. John Storseth was born in Hemne, Norway, in 1863. He emigrated to America in 1887 and settled in Poulsbo two years later. Not all immigrants reserved Norwegian place-names. Storseth mentions that immigrants from northern Norway east of Poulsbo did not find a Norwegian name for their settlement. Rangvald Kvelstad, "John Storseth: Poulsbo Pioneer," in Kitsap County Historical Society, *North Kitsap of Kitsap County History* (Seattle: Dinner & Klein, 1977), 36–37; John Storseth, "Fra gammel og ny Tid i Norge og Amerika," *Decorah-Posten,* 2 March 1944; Kvelstad, *Poulsbo,* 44–49, 62.
18. According to a letter written to *Skandinaven* in 1891, several landowning fishermen from Puget Island fished for tuna in the winter. They worked on steamers that had their stopping place at Clifton, about thirty miles from Astoria. Letter in *Decorah-Posten,* 15 March 1892; Letters in *Skandinaven,* 15 January 1890, 22 January 1890, 26 March 1890, 11 March 1891, 8 July 1891; Bjork, *West of the Great Divide,* 551, 557; Lise Lindbæk, "Tusen norske bor på Puget Island i Columbia River, hvor de laget et norsk-amerikansk 'Holland,'" *Nordisk Tidende* 4 May 1944.
19. According to an observer, the history of the island is linked to the "interplay between the Columbia River and the gigantic Pacific Ocean." Lindbæk, *Nordisk Tidende,* 4 May 1944; "Puget Island, WA," Wahkiakum Chamber of Commerce, accessed 11 July 2024, https://wahkiakum.us/visitor-info/puget-island/; "The Heritage of Heritage Bible Church," Heritage Bible Church, accessed 11 July 2024, https://www.hbcpugetisland.com/about-heritage-bible-church.html.
20. At the time of the arrival of the first immigrants from South Helgeland, Puget Island had a population of 200. At its height, the population was 600. Johansen, *Norske øyværinger i Columbia River,* 9–11.
21. According to local informants, between forty and fifty Norwegian fishermen participated in the Alaska fisheries in the 1830s. Many of them participated in the fisheries in Cook's Inlet, a fjord that was similar to the fjord landscape in Norway. Johansen, 59–65.
22. Lise Lindbæk, "Tusen norske bor på Puget Island i Columbia River, hvor de laget et norsk-amerikansk 'Holland,'" *Nordisk Tidende,* 18 May 1944; Johansen, *Norske øyværinger i Columbia River,* 49. The Norse Hall of the Helgeland Lodge was built in 1937. The diking district strives to keep the island dry. "Puget Island, WA," Wahkiakum Chamber of Commerce, accessed 11 July 2024, https://wahkiakum.us/visitor-info/puget-island/.

23. At the time, a majority of all the Norwegians were living on Puget Sound and along the Columbia River, in addition to the agricultural regions of east central Washington. Bjork, *West of the Great Divide,* 632.
24. Norwegians represented 8,334 of the 21,413 Scandinavians and of the 90,004 foreign-born people in Washington state in 1890, whereas Swedes numbered 10,272 and Danes 2,807. Bjork, *West of the Great Divide,* 632.
25. Rasmussen, *New Land, New Lives,* 7–8.
26. Barkan, *From All Points,* 69–74, 175.
27. Barkan, 71, 257.
28. The relationship between the Norwegians and the local Suquamish nation was amicable, but they lived separate lives and rarely mixed. In a centennial book on Poulsbo published in 1886, Dan Johnson, born in 1897 as the son of Norwegian immigrants, remembered how as a boy he saw Suquamish people come paddling to Dogfish Bay to dig for clams and oysters. He also saw flotillas of Vancouver Island Indigenous people coming to pick hops. Some Native Americans shared the impression of good relations between Scandinavian settlers and the Indigenous population. In an interview with the *Kitsap County Herald,* Martha George of the Suquamish nation said, "My family had no trouble whatsoever. . . . We were treated like humans by the whites." Diane Hodges, interview with Martha George in the Visitors Edition of the *Kitsap County Herald,* cited in Kvelstad, *Poulsbo,* 23.
29. Kvelstad, *Poulsbo,* 187–88.
30. Scandinavian names of various origins also appear on a list of fishing boats involved in the codfish industry out of Poulsbo and the shores of Liberty Bay. Kvelstad, *Poulsbo,* 60, 70, 155.
31. See also Dag Blanck, "Friends and Neighbors? Patterns of Norwegian-Swedish Interaction in the United States," in *Norwegian and Swedes in the United States: Friends & Neighbors,* ed. Philip J. Anderson and Dag Blanck (St. Paul: Minnesota Historical Society Press, 2011), 9.
32. For example, the fact that Poulsbo was widely known as "Norwegian." All Norwegian settlements around Puget Sound joined a common Seventeenth of May parade in Poulsbo. John Storseth, "Fra gammel og ny Tid i Norge og Amerika," *Decorah-Posten,* 17 February 1944.
33. Kathleen Neils Conzen, "Mainstreams and Side Channels: The Localization of Immigrant Cultures," *Journal of American Ethnic History* 11, no. 1 (Fall 1991): 6–15.
34. The Sigvald Quale Silver Medal contest was an ambulatory event held at various teaching institutions in the nation. It had been held in Poulsbo at least twice because Norwegian recently had been introduced in the curriculum of Poulsbo High School. Kristine Haugen, "Blandt Folket vort ude ved Soleglad," *Decorah-Posten,* 22 March 1940; A. Louis Elmquist, "New Notes," *Scandinavian Studies and Notes* 4, no. 1 (February 1917): 87.
35. Poulsbo is presented with the fictive name of Port Haven in the study. Angelo Anastasio, "Poulsbo: A Community of Transition," cited in Kitsap County Historical Society, *North Kitsap of Kitsap County History,* 18–20.
36. See, for example, Henrik Olav Mathiesen, "The Epistolary Practices of Norwegian Emigrants and the Emergence of a Transatlantic Public Sphere, ca. 1835–1870" (PhD diss., University of Oslo, 2021), 19, 411–20.

37. Vinland, the name of the Lutheran Church, is tied to Leif Erikson landing on the North American continent, which offers another parallel between colonization and settlement among Norse and Norwegian settlers. I. H. Myrvang, "Vort Folk ved Havet," *Decorah-Posten,* 4 February 1943, 11 February 1943.
38. An ardent critic of the Nazi regime, Lindbæk had fled Europe following the German occupation and finally settled in the United States. Here, she worked as a journalist in *Nordisk Tidende* and taught at two universities in the Midwest—the University of Wisconsin–Madison and the University of Minnesota in the Twin Cities. She also was very engaged in the cause of the war sailors. Sigrun Slapgard, *Krigens penn. Ein biografi om Lise Lindbæk* (Oslo: Gyldendal, 2003), 197–200; Sigrun Slapgard, "Lise Lindbæk," Norsk Biografisk Leksikon, 20 June 2024, https://nbl.snl.no/Lise_Lindb%C3%A6k; Lise Lindbæk, "Tusen norske bor på Puget Island," *Nordisk Tidende,* 4 May 1944, 18 May 1944.
39. At the time, a thousand inhabitants lived on the island, of whom 95 percent were Norwegian-American. Lise Lindbæk, "Tusen norske bor på Puget Island," *Nordisk Tidende,* 4 May 1944, 18 May 1944.
40. Norwegian recipes such as lefse and lutefisk were still in use for festive occasions, and inhabitants had a few extra red-letter days, including the Seventeenth of May. Alfred Apsler, "Little Norway On Puget Island," *Sunday Oregonian Magazine,* 6 December 1953. According to an observer, the Norwegian language on Puget Island had been rapidly disappearing ten years earlier. See Lise Lindbæk, "Tusen norske bor på Puget Island," *Nordisk Tidende,* 18 May 1944.
41. Johansen, *Norske øyværinger i Columbia River,* 49.
42. Kraut exemplifies the negotiation process by reflecting upon the health and the body of the immigrant. It is within the confines of the body as contested terrain that the process of identity negotiation between native-born and newcomers occurs most clearly. Alan M. Kraut, "Doing as Americans Do: The Post-Migration Negotiation of Identity in the United States," *Journal of American History* 101, no. 3 (December 2014): 709–11. In a similar context, Paul Connerton treats memory as a cultural faculty where ritual performances convey and sustain images of the past and argues that the performative memory is bodily. See Paul Connerton, *How Societies Remember* (Cambridge: Cambridge University Press, 1989).
43. Brian J. Godfrey, "New Ethnic Landscapes: Place Making in Urban America," in *Contemporary Ethnic Geographies in America,* ed. Christopher A. Airriess (2007; repr., Lanham, MD: Rowman & Littlefield, 2016), 61.
44. Anthony D. Smith, *The Ethnic Origins of Nations* (Malden, MA: Blackwell, 1986), 174–75, 183.
45. Smith, *Ethnic Origins of Nations,* 13–16, 183.
46. Barbro Klein, "'Treasures from the Homeland?' Om traditionsbyggen, kulturarvspolitik och Svensk-Amerika," in *Report from the Symposium "Amerika tur och retur" in Gothenburg, September 18–19, 1997, Göteborgs-Emigranten 6* (Uddevalla: Göteborgs-Emigranten, 1997), 114–28.

TEACHING AND LEARNING

Dialectal Development and Comparison

NORWEGIAN DIALECTS IN THE UNITED STATES AND NORWAY

Helen White

Norwegian has a rather well-documented history that is worth examining, both because of the novelty of many of the language's developments and because of the particular sociopolitical factors influencing the language.[1] Norwegian developed from Proto-Indo-European, then Proto-Germanic, both ancient languages, and more recently from Old Norse. Modern Norwegian has been spoken since around the year 1525, though, as any language, Norwegian has undergone a multitude of changes from above and below, or, in other words, changes influenced by both elite and rural speakers.[2] There are only two regions in which Norwegian-speaking communities of notable size have lived and operated: Norway itself and the American Midwest. The former is the birthplace of the language, and the latter was the homeplace of waves of immigrants arriving in the United States from Norway primarily between the late nineteenth to early twentieth centuries.

This sudden separate but parallel coexistence of the Norwegian language had fascinating results that can be categorized and examined today. Norwegian settlers left for the American plains in the midst of a linguistic crisis that was taking place in their homeland, meaning they did not experience the reforms and revisions that Norwegian underwent during that time period. Their language became reminiscent of a time past as they passed their language down to their children and grandchildren in the new country. Here we see a divide, a branching off that creates linguistic circumstances ripe for inquiry. Many scholars, most notably Einar Haugen and Janne Bondi Johannessen, have dedicated years to the examination of American Norwegian and its phenomena. Of the existing research, the prevailing finding regarding the impact Norwegian dialects had on one another is that American Norwegian has undergone an incomplete leveling process, meaning that the dialects have influenced one another toward a middle ground, but that variation still exists.[3]

In this research, I set out to examine the changes that the Norwegian language underwent in both the United States and Norway. Because there already existed a rich history of dialectal variation in Norway, the immigrants were often exposed to new varieties of Norwegian that they had never heard in their country of origin. Within these American communities, they often formed dialect groupings that resulted in a popular dialect that varied depending on the region in North America. Meanwhile, in Norway, an ongoing linguistic revolution brought about new recognition and status assigned to these more rural dialects, and they gained prestige that had not formerly been assigned to them. Though heritage Norwegian has become moribund in the American Midwest, examples of this preserved Norwegian form of the immigrant variety can be compared with the modern dialects of Norway to trace changes and fossilization within the language use of these two areas.

The purpose of these inquiries is to shed light on the rural dialects of both the United States and Norway and to trace general trends within language change in communities like the Norwegian-American communities that were so prevalent during the late nineteenth and early twentieth centuries. Learning more about language change can help us understand more recent linguistic developments in European Norwegian, in particular concerning dialect variation in native speakers of modern Norwegian. Acknowledging the importance—and creation—of Norwegian heritage that lives on in the cultural practices of the Midwest (i.e., in a postvernacular form) highlights the intricate connection between language (in the largest sense) and identity. My goal for this research is to determine whether Norwegian in the United States is fossilized or whether the proximity to novel dialects not encountered by these individuals in Norway has influenced their language production over a few generations. More specifically, I ask: Is Norwegian in the United States truly a relic of times gone by? Is it a preserved specimen of the Norwegian that was spoken at the time of immigration? Or is it an amalgamation of dialectal contact in a new setting for Norwegian?

In order to effectively engage with these questions and others, I have examined dialect change by combing through transcripts of interviews with heritage Norwegian speakers, found in tapes made by Terje M. H. Joranger and Odd S. Lovoll and archived in the Corpus of American Nordic Speech (CANS).[4] In these transcripts, I have found select dialectal features that shed light on how Norwegian dialects have influenced one another among Norwegian Americans. I hope to investigate whether the data found in Joranger and Lovoll in particular, as it has remained largely untouched for the past two decades, displays the incomplete leveling process as found in the research in the volume *Germanic Heritage Languages in North America: Acquisition, Attrition and Change,* edited by Janne Bondi Johannessen and Joseph C. Salmons.[5] My hypothesis is that the majority Norwegian dialect in each community in North America will influence individual respondents to speak more like the popular dialect, though elements of their heritage dialect will be maintained.

My first task will be to give some historical background about Norwegian and the sociopolitical factors that have influenced its speakers for generations. This will be particularly relevant for those who are unfamiliar with the Norwegian language or with Norwegian history in general. This history will include both the linguistic environment in Norway that the immigrants left behind and the new environments that they created upon their arrival. Next, I will describe my data sources, in particular the archival recordings housed at the Norwegian American Historical Association (NAHA) and how I matched these interviews to transcripts from CANS. I will give some demographic information about the informants and explain my process in extracting meaningful dialect data from the raw interviews. Then I will exemplify the dialect features I was looking for in the interviews, especially for those unfamiliar with Norwegian dialects. Next, I will present my data and results in a quantitative form. I will subsequently place my research in the context of current scholarship and discuss past findings about the influence of English on American Norwegian. I will compare modern Norwegian to American Norwegian and make conjectures about the sociolinguistic implications of this research. I will also include the limitations of this study. Finally, I will make some concluding remarks and suggestions for further research. At the end of this article is an appendix including a legend for the International Phonetic Alphabet notation used in this article.[6] The references may also be found at the end of the article.

History

Linguistic History and Revolution in Norway

In order to attain a fuller understanding of the context of the Norwegian language during the time of Norwegian emigration, we must first investigate the historical status of Norwegian dialects. Though this article focuses primarily on spoken Norwegian, some information about the development of standardized written forms of Norwegian is needed, as this was a huge social debate at the time that affected the prestige of local dialects of Norwegian and changed how the immigrants thought about their own language use. Additionally, some of the changes being made to Norwegian were happening after many of the immigrants had already departed, meaning they were removed from the sociolinguistic context that caused changes in modern Norwegian that did not then happen in American Norwegian. In order to trace these changes, we must investigate the history of Norwegian and, in particular, how dialects were perceived.

The history of Norwegian can be traced back to common ancestors of Germanic languages. Regarding modern Norwegian, its history is dated to 1537 with the Danish rule of Norway. In this year, Norway and Denmark became one country, under one Danish king, King Christian III of Denmark-Norway.[7] During this time period, as would be expected, the Norwegian language became heavily influenced by Danish, particularly in written form. At this time, some written language existed for Norwegian, and it was a separate entity from Danish and Swedish, which all descend from Old Norse.[8] Through Danish rule, the existing written Norwegian language was gradually replaced by written Danish.[9] As a consequence of Danish nobles and royals residing in the nation's capital, Christiania (now known as Oslo), the spoken language in the city and the surrounding areas began resembling written Danish with Norwegian phonological features. As Ernst Håkon Jahr writes of this period, "This upper-class oral variety was clearly non-Danish in terms of prosody, phonology and syntax, the word forms, morphology and vocabulary had been derived from the written Danish of the eighteenth century."[10] While this was the case of the upper class, who had the prestige that came with this Dano-Norwegian language, "fishermen's dialects were considered to be of low social status and were thus only used locally."[11] Prior to the Norwegian linguistic revolution, "there was a gradual shading off of dialects, with the lower classes in the cities speaking a language that approximated more nearly that of the surrounding countryside."[12] Dialect was heavily associated with societal status as a result of Danish colonization, where the very richest were likely of Danish origin.

In 1814, the Norwegian people were seeking independence from the rule of Denmark, writing their constitution that is still in use today. Rather than being freed from a foreign monarchy, Norway was passed from Danish rule to a union with Sweden. However, Norway could now select its own king and keep its own constitution. During this period, there was a great push of nationalism, and debates on language represented the sociopolitical division. On one end of the spectrum were those who advocated for Dano-Norwegian to become the standardized Norwegian language, arguing for the social status it had historically enjoyed and hoping to spread this supposedly high-class language to the peasants of Norway. On the other side were those who wanted to return to the roots of Norwegian, those who rejected Dano-Norwegian as a valid form of Norwegian because of the simple fact of its Danish influence, and who wanted to highlight the traditionally so-called low-class dialects of fishermen and peasants.

These two sides were represented by Knud Knudsen and Ivar Aasen, two figures of language reform during the nineteenth century. Knudsen was a staunch advocate of Dano-Norwegian, publishing a grammar text in 1856 entitled *Handbook of Dano-Norwegian Grammar.*[13] This written variety, retaining the Danish influence, would become known as Riksmål (language of the kingdom) and, from 1929 onward, Bokmål (book language). Bokmål remains the majority written form of Norwegian today. Spoken forms similar to Bokmål (though this is a written standard) are and have historically been prevalent in Eastern Norway, known as Østlandet, because of the cultural hub of Oslo/Christiania. The Danish influence is clear in this region because it was the historical residence of the Danish nobles during the Danish rule of Norway.

Figure 1. Image of Knud Knudsen (1812–1885), advocate for the use of Dano-Norwegian. Cappelen. (n.d.). Courtesy of Wikimedia Commons, https://commons.wikimedia.org/wiki/File:Knudknudsen.jpg.

Figure 2. 1895 portrait of Ivar Aasen, creator of the written form of Norwegian now known as Nynorsk. Courtesy of Nasjonalbiblioteket, https://www.nb.no/items/05ec0373c1add04e5df01df40dc2a5c1.

Ivar Aasen is a famous figure within the linguistic revolution for his advocacy for the return of Norwegian to its Old Norse roots. Aasen rejected the validity of Dano-Norwegian as a candidate for the Norwegian written standard because it was too close to Danish and did not reflect the spoken language of the Norwegian people.[14] His response was to travel around the country and conduct research on the rural dialects he felt represented a more authentic form of Norwegian, supposedly free from Danish influence. From 1842 to 1846 he published his findings in a book entitled *Det norske Folkesprogs Grammatik* [Grammar of the Norwegian dialects] as a nationalistic endeavor to create a new written variety of Norwegian.[15] This was pioneering work in the recording of Norwegian dialects and gave social status and credence to these rural varieties for the first time.

From his work, Aasen created Landsmål (country language), aiming to create a "national written standard [that] could be based directly on the dialects."[16] His motivation was based on the "idea that the national language of Norway should act as a common denominator for all rural, low-status dialects, to the exclusion of the spoken variety of the upper-middle classes," which inspired his variety to be adopted by the Norwegian people alongside Riksmål.[17] Aasen published more works using his newly developed Landsmål during the middle of the nineteenth century, and his written variety gained popularity among these rural populations.[18] Landsmål later became known as Nynorsk (new Norwegian) and is still in official use today, though it remains a minority language. The dialectal forms represented in Nynorsk are still in use today, and Nynorsk in its written form is most commonly used in more rural, northern regions of Norway.

The controversies around Bokmål and Nynorsk rose to prominence as a part of the nationalism movement of the nineteenth century. The creation of a national identity was important to gaining independence. In 1905, Norway became fully independent of Denmark and Sweden, becoming a sovereign nation.[19] The linguistic debates continued into the twentieth century, where both Bokmål and Nynorsk were in use. While the rural dialects were previously not on the same level as the higher-class Dano-Norwegian, in modern times they are considered to be associated with local pride. This is somewhat of a unique situation, where "local dialects enjoy a higher status and may be used more widely and freely in Norway than in most other European societies."[20]

Dialect Mixing in North America

The height of this linguistic revolution in Norway coincided with the height of Norwegian emigration. Between 1836 and 1915, over 750,000 Norwegians emigrated to the United States, which was about a third of the population of Norway at the time.[21] This large-scale emigration took place in three major waves: 1866–1873, 1880–1893, and 1900–1910, the largest being the middle wave. The vast majority of these emigrants were poor farmers from rural areas of Norway who were attracted to the United States by the prospect of settling farmland in the American Midwest. Given the years of departure, we can see that many of these emigrants were leaving while Aasen's linguistic reforms were taking hold and while these debates were at the forefront of the national conversation. This means that many of the immigrants brought with them linguistic varieties of the time that were consequently passed on to their children and grandchildren, while those who remained in Norway experienced the effects of the linguistic revolution that was still unfolding. This split provides a very interesting perspective on how Norwegian developed in two separate contexts.

From the beginning of when Norwegian was spoken in the United States and Canada, there existed a level of linguistic mixing between the Norwegian dialects, and now English as well. Einar Haugen, whose seminal works coined our understanding of American Norwegian, notes that "those who were freshly arrived from Norway . . . seem to have agreed from the beginning that the speech of their countrymen in America was both barbarous and confusing."[22] Suddenly, many were exposed to Norwegian dialects they had never heard in their fatherland due to geographic isolation, and this sparked language change among the immigrants. As Haugen writes: "One of the first effects of emigration was to wipe out the isolation and thereby to upset the delicate balance of dialect against dialect which was conditioned by the social geography of the old country. Speakers whose ancestors rarely had communicated in the course of a thousand years were suddenly thrown into close contact in an American community."[23] However, many also managed to keep their native dialects fairly isolated, as "the tendency was toward the resettling of old friends, neighbors, and relatives" in the new country.[24] These more dialectically separate settlements were often smaller. Haugen notes that the family was the linguistic core of the dialect, where "the family was the natural unit in the [linguistic] development that could endure for at least a while against the different opposing directions in the larger society."[25]

The meeting of these dialects in the new country gave birth to the Bygdelag movement, which allowed for the development of local pride surrounding the village in Norway where one's family had originated. This created a sense of pride around one's unique origin. Haugen notes that "the village dialects that came to create a nucleus in the old settlements had a lot in common; they were Ivar Aasen's 'real' dialects, those who, as a consequence, had held onto old Norwegian's sound system and vocabulary."[26] In Norway and especially in the United States, where these long-standing geographic boundaries were broken, "one conspicuous fact about each person was his dialect."[27] However, because of the time that the immigrants left Norway, they often did not have the same sense of pride around their dialect because of the prevalence of Dano-Norwegian during the time they left their home country. Haugen writes: "The implied standard against which the local dialects are often judged is that of the written [Dano-Norwegian] or of the corresponding spoken forms, particularly of urban dwellers in the eastern cities. From their pastors and other educated leaders they had learned that this was a more elegant form of Norwegian, and had in general accepted this judgment."[28] Some of the immigrants lamented the "ugliness" of their dialects in comparison to the more prestigious forms. However, the Bygdelag movement and the arrival of newer waves of Norwegian immigrants counteracted some of this negative sentiment. Over time, the prevailing sentiment was that the dialect forms were markers of being a "common person" or an "ordinary" speaker of Norwegian. Additionally, Dano-Norwegian was considered the proper form of writing Norwegian, while speaking remained characteristic of the dialect one spoke at home.

While most Norwegians settled near, and therefore married within their own dialect group, some would marry outside of their speech variety, producing a second generation who could switch between dialects depending on the situation.[29] These individuals were common of the second and third generation of immigrants and make up many of the informants used in this research. The dialects of these people, the later generations, have been subjected to many leveling influences; however, "even when these were in part the same as Norway, they were of such different weight and applied under such different circumstances that we could not expect the results to be the same."[30] This is to say that the Norwegian dialects we see in modern speakers of American Norwegian have taken on a life of their own and have developed separately from the regions in Norway from which they originated. The purpose of this research is to investigate some of the ways in which these dialects have changed or remained the same over the generations of separation they have experienced.

Today, Norwegian as a heritage language in the United States and Canada has become quite rare, as most speakers have since passed, and the language has largely not been passed down by heritage speakers. The disappearance of

American Norwegian is primarily caused by larger societal language homogenization. The recordings analyzed in this research are from some of the last people to have learned Norwegian as a first language in North America. Many were quite elderly at the time of recording, and the vast majority have since passed away without a continuation of heritage Norwegian in their descendants. Fortunately, American Norwegian was documented while fluent speakers were still alive, which leaves us with a bounty of information we can now use to draw conclusions retroactively about these forms of Norwegian.

Methods

Data Sources

At the core of this project is my investigation of a series of recordings made by Joranger and Lovoll of interviews of heritage Norwegian speakers.[31] These recordings were donated to the Norwegian American Historical Association, where I worked from 2021 to 2023. The collection includes over 130 tape-recorded interviews created from 1995 to 2002 for Lovoll's book *The Promise Fulfilled: A Portrait of Norwegian Americans Today.*[32] Some of the recordings are done in English, some in Norwegian, and some in a mixture of the two languages. Joranger and Lovoll traveled around the United States, primarily in the American Midwest, interviewing individuals with Norwegian heritage. This collection is still being processed at NAHA and is currently not available to the general public. As a part of my work with these materials, I have transcribed over twenty of these recordings and have selected fifteen to be a part of this research. Most of the interviews were between ten and twenty minutes in length.

In the transcription process, I wrote the dialect forms I heard to the best of my ability using my best approximation of how the dialect forms sounded using colloquial spellings. I selected the recordings for this research based on the recordings that were entirely or mostly in Norwegian and that I could understand the majority of. For this research, I will identify the respondents using the recording catalog name at NAHA. It is also worth noting that I am not a professional transcriptionist and that these transcriptions of these recordings were made based on my judgment and experience with Norwegian.

I wanted to analyze these recordings since they have mostly been unused in research and remain largely unexplored as a source of American Norwegian speech. Additionally, these recordings had not been transcribed and made more accessible in the twenty-plus years they have existed. By using these recordings as a data source, I have investigated a relatively new source of data while also using my knowledge of Norwegian to translate many of these recordings to be accessible to a broader audience. They proved to be a rich source that contained a wide range of individuals with heritage from various places in Norway.

Alongside Joranger and Lovoll's recordings, I gleaned data from the Corpus of American Nordic Speech, compiled by Janne Bondi Johannessen et al.[33] The corpus contains data collected by Johannessen et al. (2010–2016), alongside older data from Didrik Arup Seip and Ernst W. Selmer (1931), Einar Haugen (1942) and Arnstein Hjelde (1987, 1990, 1992). The corpus, in total, covers 268 informants from sixty-three different locations throughout the United States and Canada. The transcriptions in this corpus are presented in both orthographic and phonetic form. Similar to the data collected by Joranger and Lovoll, the recordings here are interviews with people speaking heritage Norwegian. CANS is publicly available online as a resource. It is also worth noting that the CANS transcriptions are much more developed and professional than my transcriptions of Joranger and Lovoll's work due to the sheer magnitude of the CANS project, which has been worked on by a wide range of scholars for a number of years. However, the preliminary transcriptions created by me are useful for the purposes of this dialect analysis with the selected dialect features.

Informants

For each of the fifteen recordings I selected from Joranger and Lovoll's interviews, I selected one informant from CANS. I selected the matches from CANS based on each informant's place of origin in Norway from Joranger and Lovoll. For each of these informants, I chose a matching informant from CANS who originated from the same village in Norway or within the same region. I also chose informants who were born around the same time so as to account for differences between generations of immigrants and the changes in American Norwegian

Figure 3. Screenshot of CANS showing a search of the pronoun *jeg* [I] in Norwegian. The search has returned 19,958 matches, showing the orthographic and phonetic forms of the word, meaning that the word was used 19,958 times throughout all samples found in the corpus. Image courtesy of author.

that may have occurred over time. From each source, I chose fifteen separate informants to investigate and fourteen separate interviews, as one interview from each source was with two individuals. While Joranger and Lovoll's recordings have identifying information, which I have removed from this report, CANS does not have identifying information. This means that there may be overlap between the respondents without my knowledge.

After matching each informant from Joranger and Lovoll to an informant from CANS, I examined all thirty transcriptions for evidence of the dialectal features I selected. The dialectal features included here were chosen based on frequency of tokens and variation between dialects. The features I selected included personal pronouns, question words, and the negation word *not.* I isolated personal pronouns because they represent lexical differences between dialects or specific differences between common words. As pronouns are abundant in most speech, it was not difficult to find instances of the use of these personal pronouns. Both the abundance of these forms and their lexical natures made pronouns a good baseline for dialectal comparison. Similarly, the negation adverb *ikke* [not] is found frequently in the transcripts. This adverb provides both a lexical and a phonological comparison point between dialects. Finally, I selected question words (like *what* [hva] and *why* [hvorfor]). Not all of the question words were encountered in the dataset, but most respondents used at least one question word. The variation in question words between dialects is mostly phonological, but some are lexical as well. These features were selected to get a sample of dialectal changes that were both easy to spot and representative of larger changes between varieties of Norwegian. All of the aforementioned forms will be examined and explained in depth later in the report prior to presenting the data. Isolating a few dialectal features was necessary for the purpose of being able to compare between dialects, both in American Norwegian and modern Norwegian.

For each speaker, I identified the dialect grouping (out of Østlandet [the East], Vestlandet [the West], Sørlandet [the South], and Trøndelag) to which they were most likely to belong, as well as my best estimation of what the majority dialect was in the area where they resided in North America. At times, finding this information could be challenging, and it was often dictated by what the respondent identified as the majority dialect(s) in the region. This metalinguistic information can be useful because the dialects named by the respondents are most likely to have had the biggest influence on the respondent's actual speech, as the speakers are most aware of these dialects. However, respondents may be incorrect when providing this information and may have a skewed perception of the demographic information of the area. After I had identified which dialect grouping best suited the individual and the community to which they belonged, I found which dialect forms best matched both of these categorizations and compared these forms to the forms used by the respondent. In this manner, I was able to identify which forms the respondent had retained from their family's region of origin in Norway and which forms had been influenced by the majority dialect of the region in the United States. Some forms remained unexplained by either of these factors.

Dialect Groupings

Finally, I used several scholarly studies to inform my investigation. Much of the present scholarship examines the effect of English on American Norwegian, and studies about the dialectal variation in American Norwegian are rather sparse. Much of the relevant literature comes from Ernst Håkon Jahr and Janne Bondi Johannessen more recently and Einar Haugen in the mid-twentieth century. In the comparison section of this article, I will return to scholarship on American Norwegian dialects and place the data in the larger context of the current literature on the subject. Much of their work has informed the historical background I have provided earlier and has given insight into previous findings regarding larger trends in Norwegian-American language use.

Modern dialect groupings tend to fall into four major categories, which are far broader: Østlandet, Vestlandet, Trøndelag, and Nord-Norge [the North].[34] Within American Norwegian speech, Østlandet and Vestlandet are the most represented categories of Norwegian dialects, and Nord-Norge is the least represented. Because none of the respondents I came across in Joranger and Lovoll's interviews had heritage from anywhere farther north than Trøndelag, I decided to omit Nord-Norge as a category from this report. The fact that this dialect is scarcely represented in American Norwegian is unsurprising because Nord-Norge is the traditional land of the Indigenous peoples in Norway and has a very small population. Instead of including a dialect region with no representative speakers, I added Sørlandet as a dialect region, in order to keep four distinctive categories. Sørlandet is at times considered to be a dialect region, but as it has much in common with Vestlandet dialect, it is often not included and is instead grouped in with Vestlandet. Therefore, my four regional dialect categories in this report are the following: Østlandet, Vestlandet, Trøndelag, and Sørlandet, which I will refer to using their Norwegian names in the remainder of this report.

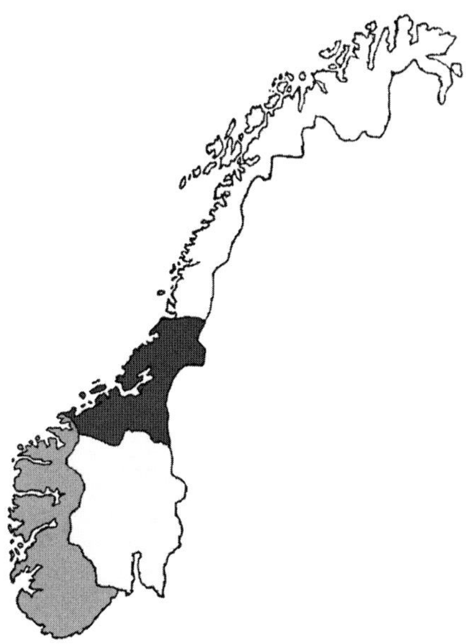

Figure 4. Traditional Norwegian dialect groupings, including Nord-Norge (top), Trøndelag (center), Østlandet (rightmost bottom), and Vestlandet (leftmost bottom). Sørlandet lies at the southernmost part of the country. Courtesy of Wikimedia Commons, https://commons.wikimedia.org/wiki/File:Norwegian_dialects.PNG.

In order to compare American Norwegian dialects to modern Norwegian dialects, sample recordings made by Jørn Almberg and Kristian Skarbø were analyzed. These recordings are publicly available through the Norwegian University of Science and Technology (Norges teknisk-naturvitenskapelige universitet, NTNU) and are housed in a database including fifty-five recordings.[35] In these recordings, informants were asked to read a source text aloud and were allowed to make changes to the text to better suit their dialects. These recordings are an excellent baseline for comparing American Norwegian speech to modern Norwegian speech. In total, I cataloged 273 unique tokens from thirty unique speakers, 135 of those being from Joranger and Lovoll and 138 of those being from CANS. For each respondent, I identified two categories in which to sort tokens: those representative of the respondent's own dialect and those that suited the majority dialect in the area in which they settled. For the respondent's own dialect, I used the areas in Norway where respondents claimed their ancestors had emigrated from. This was self-reported by the respondents, so it could contain errors, as many of these respondents were third- or fourth-generation immigrants. However, if respondents reported having ancestry from these areas, they likely identified with this region and perhaps, by extension, the dialect spoken there. The idea behind this category is that if respondents had ancestors originating from certain areas of Norway, they would be likely to speak a dialect similar to the dialect spoken in that particular region of Norway. The other major category of investigation was the perceived majority dialect in the region in North America in which the respondent was residing. This was also self-reported, as data was not often collected on which areas of North America had residents with ancestry from certain regions of Norway. For the Joranger and Lovoll data, this was often an interview question, where the interviewer asked the respondent what areas of Norway were most commonly represented in this region of the United States. The respondent's answer informed my categorization, which often included at least two areas of Norway as being representative of the dialect spoken in that region. In the CANS data, I looked at the origin of all respondents from that town in North America and drew common areas from each respondent's self-reported region of origin in Norway. The findings were that the vast majority of respondents had a native dialect (passed down from their ancestors) that aligned with the majority dialect of the region.

Table 1. Respondent demographic information

Demographic	Number of speakers	Percentage
Male	18	60.0
Female	12	40.0
Family from Østlandet region	17	56.7
Family from Sørlandet region	2	6.7
Family from Trøndelag region	5	16.7
Family from Vestlandet region	9	30.0
Family from unknown region	2	6.7
Family from more than one region	5	16.7

Demographic information about the informants selected for this research, including gender distribution and their family's area of origin in Norway. Please note that five respondents identified two different areas of heritage each, meaning that the totals add up to forty here, a greater number than the actual number of speakers. The percentages show the percentage of respondents out of thirty (the total number of respondents) that identified as having heritage from the respective area.

In order to determine how each token fit into each category, I used multiple sources on features of Norwegian dialects. I used the dialect maps created by Martin Skjekkeland and Hallfrid Christiansen and those from Ernst Håkon Jahr's *Den store dialektboka.*[36] Finally, I listened to and read the transcripts of recordings from Almberg and Skarbø to determine which dialect forms were appropriate for both the native and the majority dialect categories. Using the data I collected, I then compared my findings to modern literature, primarily from the volume *Germanic Heritage Languages in North America: Acquisition, Attrition and Change,* edited by Janne Bondi Johannessen and Joseph C. Salmons.[37] This volume contains several contemporary studies on American Norwegian and its current status in North America that proved very useful in interpreting my results.

Data and Features

Dialect Features

In order to fully understand the data regarding dialectal variation, we must first examine the dialectal features themselves and explain some of the differences I encountered. To begin with, I compared the pronoun form used, including the object pronouns in first-person singular, third-person singular, first-person plural, and third-person plural, since these showed up most frequently in the interviews and display the most variation between dialects. As demonstrated in Table 2, the changes are largely lexical in nature, and the pronouns display a wide range of variability.

Table 2. Typical object pronoun forms comparing Bokmål, Nynorsk, and other dialectal forms

Pronoun	Bokmål	Nynorsk	Other dialectal forms
1st-person singular	‹jeg› /jæɪ/	‹eg› /e:g/	‹æ›, ‹i›, ‹e› /æ:/, /i:/, /e:/
3rd-person singular	‹han›, ‹hun› /han/, /hʉn/	‹han›, ‹ho› /han/, /hu:/	‹‘n› /n̩/
1st-person plural	‹vi› /vi:/	‹vi› /vi:/	‹me› /me:/
3rd-person plural	‹de› /di:/	‹dei› /dæɪ/	‹dem›, ‹døm› /dɛm/, /dœm/

As shown in Table 2, pronouns display a general trend based on the region of the country, with the divide being primarily between Østlandet, which historically leans more toward a spoken form of Bokmål, and Vestlandet, which leans more toward dialect forms. These maps were used to determine whether or not the respondents used the dialect form appropriate to the region in Norway that they originated from.

Another prominent dialectal feature I chose to investigate was the negation adverb *ikke* [not]. The varying forms of this adverb are displayed in Table 3. The differences between these forms are largely phonological, as can be seen in their written forms. The main difference is whether or not the word contains some sort of fricative sound, namely /ʃ/, as indicated by the addition of the *j*. The differences were notably subtler for this adverb than for the pronouns, but they provided a useful phonetic baseline, as many dialects that include the /ʃ/ sound in this word include it in other words with a /k/ sound as well.

Table 3. Forms of the negation adverb *ikke* in Bokmål, Nynorsk, and other dialectal forms

Bokmål	Nynorsk	Other dialectal forms
‹ikke› /ɪʃə/	‹ikkje› /ɪʃə/	‹ittj›, ‹itte›, ‹inte› /ɪʈʂ/, /ɪtə/, /ɪntə/

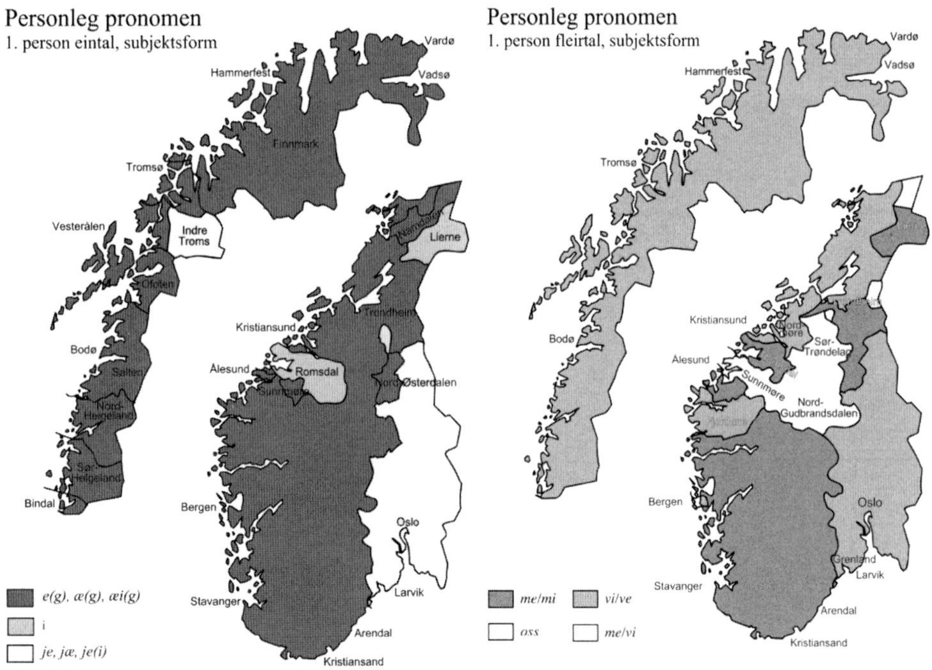

Figure 5. Map of first-person singular (*left*) and plural (*right*) pronoun distribution. Mapping of dialect forms of the first-person singular pronoun developed by Martin Skjekkeland and Hallfrid Christiansen, available at Kjell Venås and Martin Skjekkeland, "Dialekter i Noreg," Store Norske Leksikon, 23 January 2023, https://snl.no/dialekter_i_Noreg.

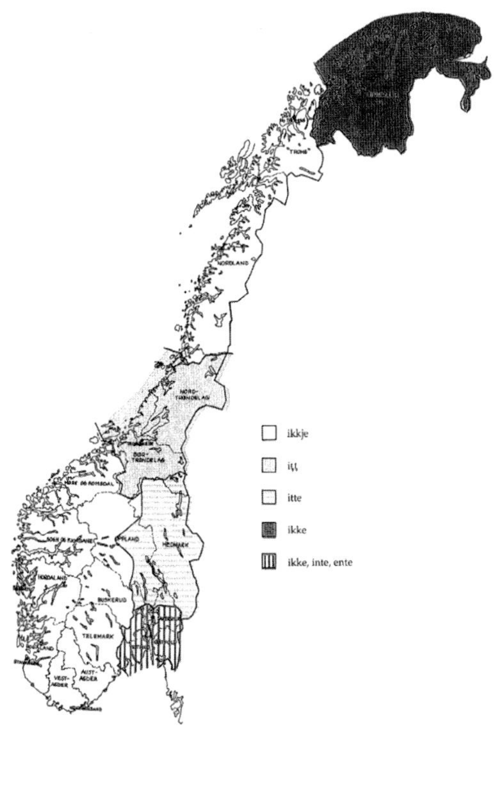

Figure 6. Map of negation adverb variation. Map of the distribution of the negation adverb *ikke* taken from Ernst Håkon Jahr.

Finally, I investigated the variation in question words. As many question words in English begin with the same sound, so do many question words in Norwegian, typically "hv" (/v/) or "k" (/k/). Table 4 illustrates the differences in these sets of question words.

Table 4. Question words in Norwegian, comparing English, Bokmål, Nynorsk, and other dialects

English	Bokmål	Nynorsk	Other dialectal forms
what	‹hva› /va:/	‹kva› /kva:/	‹ka›, ‹kå›, ‹hå› /ka:/, /kɔ:/, /hɔ:/
who	‹hvem› /vɛm/	‹kven› /kvɛn/	‹kem›, ‹håkken› /kɛm/, /hɔkn̩/
where	‹hvor› /vu:r/	‹kvar› /kva:r/	‹kor›, ‹kvor›, ‹hår› /ku:r/, /kvu:r/, /hɔ:r/
why	‹hvorfor› /vu:rfur/	‹kvifor› /kvi:fur/	‹kofför›, ‹kvorfor›, ‹håfør› /kofœr/, /kvu:rfur/, /hɔ:fœr/
how	‹hvordan› /vu:rdan̩/	‹korleis› /ku:rlæɪs/	‹kordan›, ‹håssen›, ‹åssen› /ku:rdan̩/, /hɔsn̩/, /ɔsn̩/
which	‹hvilken›, ‹hvilket› /vɪlkɛn̩/, /vɪlkɛ/	‹kossen› /kʊsɛn̩/	—
each	‹hver› /væ:r/	‹kor› /ku:r/	—

These question words often come in sets, as seen above. For example, if one speaker says *kva* for "what," they are likely to also say *kvar* for "where." This distinction is somewhat lexical, as some of the question words vary greatly, for example between *hvordan* and *korleis* for "how," but there is a systemic phonological shift from "hv" (/v/) to "kv" (/kv/) occurring here, which extends beyond just the question words. Again, we see a clear baseline for comparison that allows for examination and categorization of the data collected.

Data and Results

Using the methods described earlier, I searched the selected transcripts for the dialect forms as described above. Table 5 provides a statistical summary of my categorization of the data as explained in my methods.

Table 5. Token count statistical summary

Group	Average number of unique tokens	Tokens representative of respondent's own dialect	Tokens representative of majority dialect in region	Tokens unexplained by own dialect or majority dialect
Lovoll and Joranger data	9.0	69.1% (6.1)	85.6% (7.6)	12.6% (1.3)
CANS data	9.2	79.8% (7.0)	96.6% (8.9)	3.6% (0.4)
Heritage from Østlandet	8.6	82.2% (6.9)	97.1% (8.6)	2.1% (0.2)
Heritage from Sørlandet	10.0	75.0% (7.5)	87.5% (9.0)	12.5% (1.0)
Heritage from Trøndelag	8.2	75.4% (6.0)	90.9% (7.4)	9.1% (0.8)
Heritage from Vestlandet	10.0	61.0% (6.1)	83.8% (8.2)	14.8% (1.7)
Heritage from unknown region	10.5	N/A	93.8% (10.0)	N/A
Heritage from >1 region	9.2	77.7% (7.0)	97.8% (9.2)	2.2% (0.2)
Overall averages	**9.1**	**74.4% (6.5)**	**91.1% (8.2)**	**8.1% (0.8)**

Statistical summary of token data collected from Joranger and Lovoll and CANS (absolute numbers in parentheses). The numbers above represent the averages for each respective category. The percentages are averages showing how much of each individual's speech was representative of their own dialect, their majority dialect, and how much was unknown.

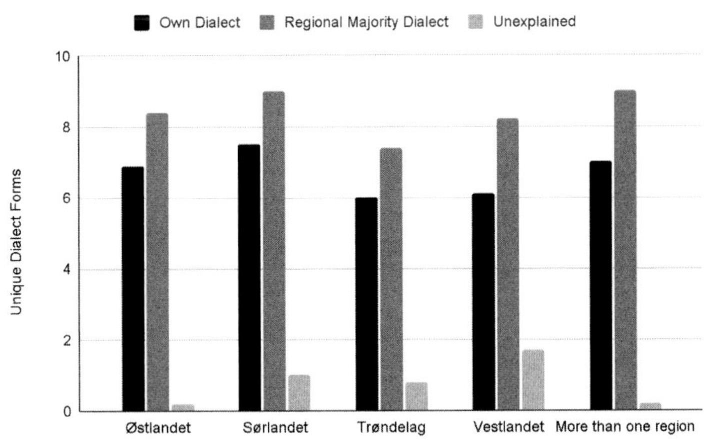

Figure 7. Graph of token distribution. Graphic representation of Table 5 showing the number of tokens representing the regional majority dialect, the number of tokens representing the respondent's own heritage dialect, and the number of tokens left unexplained. The bars show averages for each category.

As demonstrated by Table 5, there is a trend of influence from the majority dialect onto the tokens used by respondents. Figure 7 shows how the majority dialect aligns more with respondent speech than the heritage dialect. The heritage dialect has a strong influence: over 50 percent of the tokens, on average, align with the heritage dialect. However, the regional majority dialect, as an innately broader category that describes speech trends among an entire group rather than one individual, encompasses more of the respondent speech. Since the respondents are often several generations removed from their original heritage dialect, it makes sense that the regional majority dialect would have a strong influence on respondent speech. It is worth noting that of the thirty respondents, twenty-five were majority dialect speakers, two had a background from one area represented in the majority dialect but also had a background from another area not represented in the majority dialect, one did not have a background from the majority dialect, and two were unknown. This means that most respondents were a part of communities that were clusters of people with heritage from the same region of Norway. In other words, most respondents came from the region in Norway where the majority Norwegian-American population in their local area also came from. As a result, we would expect to see the majority dialect reinforcing the native dialect of the speaker and, therefore, a high percentage of tokens representing the respondent's own native dialect. However, we must take into consideration the fact that the majority dialect often includes multiple areas of Norway and thus multiple dialectal features. Because this majority dialect is a larger category than the native dialect of the speaker, the percentage of tokens representative of the majority dialect is higher than the percentage of tokens representative of the native dialect in all participants examined.

Some tokens remain unexplained but could be attributed to a variety of causes. Because these respondents were often third- or fourth-generation heritage speakers of Norwegian, they likely had many different sources of Norwegian that informed their dialect. Most of them did not receive any formal schooling in Norwegian, though some received some parochial education in the language. Because of this, they relied almost exclusively on input from other heritage speakers, or perhaps some native speakers such as their grandparents, to inform their language development. Perhaps some of them had one grandparent from Østlandet and one from Vestlandet, resulting in a dialect that mixes forms from both regions. Some respondents had no unexplained tokens, meaning they adhered more strictly to what one might expect in their native dialect or in the majority dialect, while others had several unexplained tokens, meaning they might have had more diverse influences on their language development, such as a close family member who had ancestry from a different region. Additionally, while many of the respondents were native to the area in North America where they currently resided, some of them had moved and talked about their parents or grandparents also initially settling in one area and then relocating to another. This would likely also affect language development. However, it becomes impossible to pinpoint and isolate all of these influences, leaving some tokens unexplained.

In particular, it seemed that the third-person plural pronoun (*they*) was unstable: eight out of the thirty speakers (26.7 percent) had that pronoun as one of their unexplained tokens. Generally, the pronouns appeared to be less stable than the question words; most of the unexplained tokens consisted of pronoun forms. Table 6 breaks down which features showed the most variation. For each speaker, I identified the features in which more than one form was used by the same speaker. This demonstrates that the feature is unstable within the respondent's speech and might be more subject to influence from outside dialects.

We can see from Table 6 and Figure 8 that the plural pronouns, and in particular the third-person plural pronoun, showed the most variability among speakers. The vast majority of the respondents used more than one form of the same feature. In fact, only six (20 percent) showed no variation in their speech. This means that most of the speakers were influenced by other dialect forms and used forms belonging to multiple dialects. Those who had heritage from Vestlandet of Norway demonstrated that 22.8 percent of their tokens could be attributed to the influence of the majority dialect alone. This is the highest percentage difference between the native dialect and majority dialect categories, suggesting that respondents with heritage from this area of Norway were most likely to be

Table 6. Speaker variation by dialect feature

Group	1st singular pronoun	3rd singular pronoun	1st plural pronoun	3rd plural pronoun	Question words	Negation adverb
Heritage from Østlandet	2	3	3	7	3	4
Heritage from Sørlandet	1	0	1	2	1	1
Heritage from Trøndelag	1	1	2	3	1	0
Heritage from Vestlandet	1	1	3	6	4	2
Heritage from unknown region	1	1	2	1	0	0
Heritage from >1 region	1	0	1	2	3	2
Overall	**6**	**6**	**10**	**17**	**6**	**5**
Percentage of speakers showing variation	**20.0**	**20.0**	**33.3**	**56.7**	**20.0**	**16.7**

Table showing a breakdown of the number of speakers who showed variation (used more than one form) in dialectal features. Note that some instances come from speakers who have heritage from more than one region.

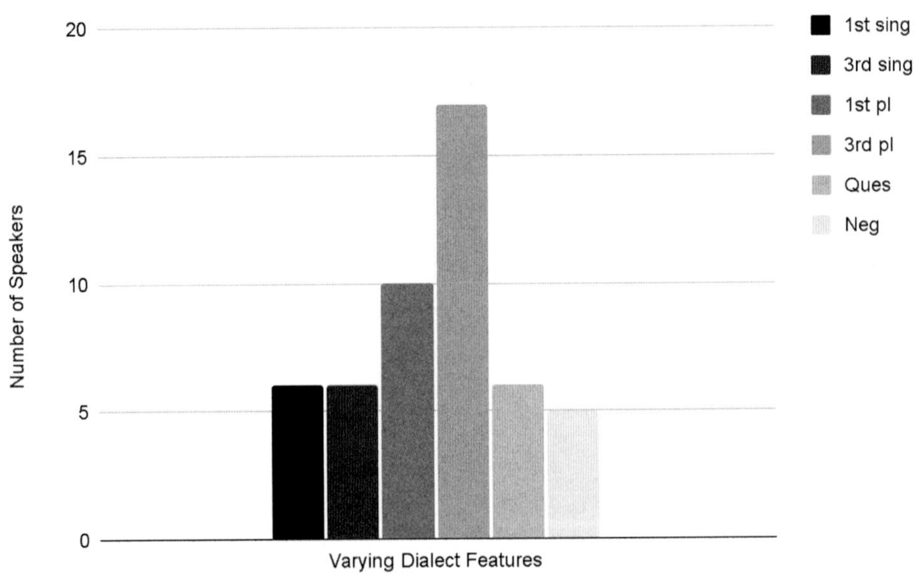

Figure 8. Graph of speaker variation. Graphic representation of Table 6 showing the distribution of the number of speakers who used two or more forms of the same dialect feature for different regions of origin in Norway. Graph shows overall numbers, not the distribution between regions as shown in Table 6.

influenced by the majority dialect in their settlement in North America. Respondents from Vestlandet also had the highest percentage of unexplained tokens, at 14.8 percent. This is likely because the Vestland dialect is the furthest away from the Østland dialect, which, of all the regions of origin, represents the majority of the respondents examined in this report. Additionally, as the most prestigious dialect at the time that many of the respondents' ancestors departed from Norway was Dano-Norwegian, heritage speakers might feel a trend toward a more Dano-Norwegian-sounding dialect, which is most reflective of the Østland dialect. Notably as well, those with family from Østlandet had the lowest percentage of unexplained token forms. Perhaps the general trend, among these respondents at least, was toward the Østland forms. The respondents with no information about their region of origin in Norway were both present in the interview with another respondent, but they did not provide this information, therefore making it impossible to give percentages to the native dialect and unexplained categories.

Additionally, one can note that the data from CANS had a higher percentages of adherence to both the native and majority dialects and that the percentage of unexplained tokens was lower than the Joranger and Lovoll data. This can be attributed to the fact that the CANS data has both orthographic and phonetic transcriptions for their interviews, while the Joranger and Lovoll data was transcribed by me and did not include a professional phonetic transcription. Because of this, the nuances of the present phonology were often not as easily accessible in the Joranger and Lovoll recordings. Since I am not a trained transcriptionist, I was not able to phonetically transcribe the recordings the way they were done in CANS, which likely explains the disparity between these two groups.

There was also a great deal of mixing dialect forms, which was of particular interest. Many speakers used more than one form for pronouns and question words, flipping back and forth between a form typical of one dialect region to another. This is unusual in native Norwegian speakers, who are typically raised in environments where one dialect form wins out. This fact supports the theory that many of these heritage speakers have mixed dialects because of multiple influences on their language development. Because they are using conflicting dialect forms, they are demonstrating conflicting dialectal development and influence.

Discussion

Contemporary Literature on American Norwegian

Much of the contemporary comparative literature comes from the volume *Germanic Heritage Languages in North America: Acquisition, Attrition and Change,* edited by Janne Bondi Johannessen and Joseph C. Salmons.[38] Johannessen herself is one of the main contributors to CANS and so has written relevant studies using this data. In particular, the chapter "On Two Myths of the Norwegian Language in America: Is It Old-Fashioned? Is It Approaching the Written Bokmål Standard?" by Janne Bondi Johannessen and Signe Laake is poignant concerning the comparison of American Norwegian to modern Norwegian.[39] For this study, the authors selected four informants from the Gudbrandsdalen area of Norway, located in Østlandet. Some of the informants in this report have heritage from this very same subregion. Johannessen and Laake found that among these informants, their Norwegian was not archaic, except perhaps at the lexical level. However, the grammar was notably similar to the dialect of origin, in this case from Gudbrandsdalen. Regarding American Norwegian's similarity to Bokmål, Johannessen and Laake point out that modern Bokmål contained more dialect forms than the older Riksmål mentioned earlier in this report but that "at no point is American Norwegian closer to Bokmål than to the Gausdal dialect."[40] Most important to this report, Johannessen and Laake conclude that "when it comes to pronouns and function words, we saw some examples of variation that suggest that American Norwegian has elements from more than one Norwegian dialect area."[41] The study conducted by Johannessen and Laake aligns with the findings of the present report in that American Norwegian has often been influenced by multiple dialects.

However, the question then rises: How have these dialects changed over time? Do they resemble modern Norwegian? Have they undergone some of the same changes that Norwegian in Norway has? Johannessen and Laake introduce the concept of a koine, suggesting that "the language of Norwegian Americans has undergone an incomplete koniéization process."[42] The koine is defined (with the context of American Norwegian) in the chapter "Changes in a Norwegian Dialect in America," written by Arnstein Hjelde, from the same volume edited by Johannessen and Salmons:

> There are reasons to believe that this process has not followed the same paths in all Norwegian-American communities: Some settlements were established by people from a rather small area in Norway and where everybody spoke the same dialect when they settled. Others were populated by people from different places in Norway, speaking a greater range of dialects. It is fair to assume that in the first case, the dialects did not change much except for changes due to contact with English. On the other hand, in communities where different dialects met, we should expect to find that dialect contact over time results in the formation of a "new" dialect, a koiné.[43]

Simply put, a koine is the result of the meeting of several mutually intelligible dialects that then influence each other to create a new dialect. Modern literature theorizes that such a process has happened to Norwegian spoken in North America as a result of Einar Haugen's observation that for many Norwegian emigrants, "their arrival in America meant also their first acquaintance with the more remote dialects spoken in their homeland."[44] Hjelde's investigation centered on Coon Valley, Wisconsin, a settlement with many heritage Norwegian speakers, also represented in respondents pulled from CANS in this report. The findings were that "still today there is a lot of dialectal variation in the speech of those with an East Norwegian (especially Gudbrandsdal) background."[45] In line with the findings of Johannessen and Laake, Hjelde also concluded that the koineization process is incomplete in American Norwegian. The findings of this report concur with this conclusion: if there was a complete koineization process, we would expect to see no intraspeaker variation and not much speaker variation in dialects within the same communities in North America.

Special attention is given to the Gudbrandsdal region of Norway, which is a part of Østlandet. This aligns with my findings, since the respondents with heritage from Østlandet make up the largest dialect group (56.7 percent) among my own respondents. However, enough variation existed that an incomplete leveling process still occurred, as found in the studies discussed above. Perhaps the individuals with heritage from Østlandet, particularly Gudbrandsdal, are least susceptible to other dialectal influences. This is supported by my finding that, on average, for respondents with heritage from Østlandet, 82.2 percent of the observed tokens could be attributed to the respondent's heritage dialect, a higher percentage than any other region of origin in Norway. Additionally, 97.1 percent of the observed tokens for respondents with Østlandet heritage could be attributed to the majority dialect of the North American region where the respondent was living, all of which included the Østland dialect. Clearly, in the case of American Norwegian, Østlandet largely wins out as a dialectal region.

Another study from Johannessen and Salmons' volume, entitled "Attrition in an American Norwegian Heritage Language Speaker" and conducted by Johannessen, tested the regression hypothesis in one older adult heritage Norwegian speaker.[46] The regression hypothesis posits, in short, that what is learned first is retained the longest, and what is learned most recently is lost first.[47] Essentially, when applied to heritage Norwegian in an older adult speaker, the theory was that the respondent's Norwegian abilities would mirror that of a first-language learner (L1) of native Norwegian. While some of the more complex language structures (like grammar rules that do not convey any semantic purpose) may be forgotten, the respondent would retain some of the more fundamental features of Norwegian. This change is due to a process called attrition, in which a native language is forgotten when it is no longer the majority language spoken in the environment surrounding the speaker.[48] In "Daisy," the respondent for this study, Johannessen concludes that "her heritage language production reveals language that is different both from what we know of Heritage Norwegian from other sources and from European Norwegian, and which is taken to be the result of language attrition."[49] Additionally, the regression hypothesis was supported in some areas of Daisy's speech—namely, in clause-related categories rather than noun-phrase-related categories. Johannessen notes that this is because pronouns are acquired early in L1 Norwegian speakers and are "fully in place for Daisy."[50] Language attrition definitely affects the language of the respondents used in this report. As many of them are a few generations away from their immigrant ancestors, their language has undergone changes and has ultimately been weakened with distance from the original immigration event and from lack of use. This is ultimately an important factor in considering how their dialect use might compare to that of a native Norwegian speaker.

Modern Norwegian

In comparing my data to modern Norwegian, a study from Björn Lundquist, Maud Westendorp, and Bror-Magnus S. Strand explains some of the parallel development that Norwegian dialects have undergone in Norway.[51] In this experiment, the researchers attempted to elicit code-switching in young speakers of the Tromsø dialect (in the Nord-Norge dialect grouping) by exposing them to Bokmål. They measured two experimental conditions, referred to as spoken (a researcher of the Tromsø dialect asked the respondent to verbally fill in the blank of a sentence spoken by the researcher) and written (the respondent verbally filled in the blank of a sentence written in Bokmål). They hoped to show that these speakers would code-switch to Bokmål forms during the written experiment. One of the measures of dialect forms versus standardized forms was the use of the first-person singular pronoun, which I have used in this report. The researchers also made use of the question word sounds ("hv-" versus "k-") to measure dialect and standard forms. They found that when respondents were exposed to written Bokmål, they were far more likely to use the standardized Bokmål forms in their spoken responses. Notably, even in the spoken experiment, where there was no exposure to Bokmål, respondents varied their language use between dialect forms and standardized forms. Specifically, the first-person singular pronoun proved to be more stable than the other dialect measures (which included word order and morphological endings), as 104 tokens of the Bokmål form (*jeg*) were elicited in the written experiment, while 0 tokens of the Bokmål form were recorded in the spoken experiment. For the question words, 286 tokens of the Bokmål form ("hv-" onset) were found in the written experiment, and 182 tokens of the Bokmål form were found in the spoken experiment.[52] In this experiment, the first-person pronoun was far more stable than the question word onset sound. For question words, the participants varied the onset sound, even when there was no exposure to Bokmål. For Norwegian Americans in this report, the amount of variation was the same between these two categories, but the third-person plural pronoun was more unstable than the first-person singular pronoun. Since Lundquist, Westendorp, and Strand examined only this pronoun, it is difficult to compare the findings, but what we can take away from this is that even native speakers of Norwegian vary between dialect forms. Lundquist, Westendorp, and Strand theorize as to the reason for this variation:

> In Tromsø today, as in most larger towns in Norway, we can assume that many speakers have a more mixed dialect background, even though they still often conform to the classic dialect traits of their hometown. It is therefore highly likely that the high school students of today speak a more levelled dialect compared to the speakers in the Nordic Dialect Corpus.[53]

What the study is suggesting here is parallel to what we see in scholarship on American Norwegian speech: greater dialectal contact resulting in dialect leveling and variation between differing dialect forms. At the time that many of the ancestors of the respondents in this report departed from Norway, these levels of dialectal contact within Norway did not exist, which is why many were exposed to new dialects in North America. However, it seems that with time and more robust communication methods, dialectal contact has increased within Norway itself as well, resulting in dialect leveling. It seems that our respondents vary their dialect forms more frequently than native Norwegian speakers would, based on this study, but the variation still exists within modern Norwegian dialects.

Limitations

Some key limitations to this research must be identified for further research. First, research in this area is extremely limited in terms of the number of available participants. The CANS corpus has data from a few hundred informants over decades of research on American Norwegian, but the vast majority of these respondents have since died, leaving very few speakers of heritage Norwegian in the United States today. This makes further research in the field difficult, as we must retroactively examine prior interviews rather than conducting new ones. If new interviews were to be conducted, researchers would likely have a small interviewee pool to choose from. The reality of other ethnic groups and languages prevailing in the settlements that were once primarily Norwegian-American has led to the decline of Norwegian as a heritage language. While thirty respondents from two different data sources were examined in this report, I could not ask questions firsthand that I may have wanted to, as I did not conduct the interviews. Furthermore, thirty is a relatively small sample size to be able to draw firm conclusions about heritage Norwegian in general. However, the process of combing through the interviews is arduous and time consuming, and because of time restrictions I was not able to investigate more respondents from Joranger and Lovoll or CANS.

Additionally, though interviews in CANS were already professionally transcribed both orthographically and phonetically, making it easier to pick out dialect features, the data from Joranger and Lovoll was largely untouched. I am not a professional transcriptionist, nor were the tapes of the highest audio quality, meaning that my transcripts could be prone to error. At times, the speech could be difficult to hear and interpret because of the audio quality of tapes made in the 1990s, muffled speech, antiquated Norwegian, background noise, and other audio distortions. This likely accounts for the discrepancy in data between Joranger and Lovoll and CANS as seen in Table 5. The CANS professional transcriptions are likely more accurate to the recordings than my transcriptions of Joranger and Lovoll's interviews.

Accounting for all the possible dialectal influences on a single respondent can become quite challenging. We may assume that their family has had a large impact on their language use in their upbringing, but perhaps other individuals, like family friends, teachers, and pastors, who speak a minority dialect of Norwegian have influenced the speech of some of the respondents. This explains why we might see some unexplained tokens: informants could have picked up a dialect form from a wide variety of sources that may not be recorded. It can also be quite difficult to find a definitive answer on which dialect feature belongs to which region in Norway, since dialects change over time and there is no single guide mapping out all dialect features. For example, the geographical distribution of the question word onset sound was difficult to pin down. The forms are generally agreed upon, but it can be difficult to find isoglosses of where each form is used. This made it difficult to categorize the dialects of the informants and where their speech might belong to. I tried to be more forgiving where I could and to incorporate more dialect forms into each category rather than fewer. However, mapping dialect features is not straightforward and may be inaccurate because of the increase of dialect contact in modern Norwegian. All of the aforementioned limitations mean that this data may not be entirely free from error, though the fact that it aligns with earlier research on American Norwegian is encouraging.

Conclusion

The long journey that Norwegian has taken in both North America and Norway itself has resulted in the creation of a diverse tapestry of the language. Norwegian comes in many different forms and is not constricted to one standard but instead allowed to grow and change with the people who speak it. The present report shows some of this change and measures it over time through investigation of heritage Norwegian speech, passed down from generation to generation in an environment where it is by far the minority language. In order to extrapolate upon the research questions, data from Joranger and Lovoll's mostly unused interviews and the CANS database were employed to investigate selected dialectal features in the informants that served as a proxy to determine dialectal membership. The dialectal features investigated were first and third pronoun use, question word onset sound, and the negation adverb *ikke*. The conclusions of this research are chiefly the following:

1. Heritage Norwegian has been subjected to an incomplete dialect leveling process interrupted by the introduction of English.
2. Speakers of heritage Norwegian display a great deal of variety in the dialect forms that they employ and often mix features from multiple dialects.

3. American Norwegian speech is often influenced by the majority Norwegian dialect in the region in which informants reside in North America, though their heritage dialect often plays a major role as well.
4. Modern Norwegian may be headed toward a leveling process in the same manner due to more dialectal contact in Norway today.

If possible, more research must be done on the heritage Norwegian speakers that remain in North America today, as the variety is already moribund. The extent to which speakers of modern Norwegian oscillate between dialect forms in their everyday lives and the causes of this variation must also be investigated further to understand the intricate balance along the dialect continuum. It would also be of interest to contextualize the data from Joranger and Lovoll's recordings in contemporary literature, since they have not been included very much at this time. The present methodology may also be employed on the same informants but using different dialectal markers, perhaps of a grammatical nature, in order to compare that development with the features in this report.

My hypothesis that the regional majority dialect would influence the speech of heritage Norwegian speakers was correct regarding the present data. Speakers of American Norwegian represent a minority language that is dying off after having been passed down for several generations, but it is nonetheless worth examining. What we see in these speakers are fascinating and complex linguistic influences interacting with one another to produce the speech we hear today. Even as heritage Norwegian is spoken less and less, it represents a history that these respondents clearly hold dear and displays an interesting incomplete leveling process, a case study in what happens when distinct but mutually intelligible dialects meet one another.

Helen White *is a graduate of the St. Olaf College Class of 2023, holding a bachelor's in applied linguistics and Norwegian. She has been studying Norwegian for over ten years after living abroad in her middle school years. She gained an interest in Norwegian-American studies after becoming a NAHA intern in the summer of 2021. Helen is the recipient of the 2023 Odd S. Lovoll Award for her work on this essay.*

28. Haugen, 355.
29. Haugen.
30. Haugen, 360.
31. Joranger and Lovoll, Oral Histories Collection.
32. Odd S. Lovoll, *The Promise Fulfilled: A Portrait of Norwegian Americans Today* (Minneapolis: University of Minnesota Press, 2007).
33. Janne Bondi Johannessen, “CANS: Corpus of American Nordic Speech v.3.1,” in *Proceedings of the 20th Nordic Conference of Computational Linguistics, NODALIDA 2015, May 11–13, 2015, Vilnius, Lithuania, NEALT Proceedings Series 23,* ed. Béata Megyesi, available at Norsk i Amerika, http://tekstlab.uio.no/norskiamerika/english/corpus.html.
34. Kjell Venås and Martin Skjekkeland, “Dialekter i Noreg,” Store Norske Leksikon, updated 23 January 2023, https://snl.no/dialekter_i_Noreg.
35. Jørn Almberg and Kristian Skarbø, “Nordavinden og sola: Opptak og transkripsjoner av norske dialekter,” NTNU, accessed 31 March 2023, https://www.hf.ntnu.no/nos/.
36. Kjell Venås and Martin Skjekkeland, “Dialekter i Noreg,” Store Norske Leksikon, 23 January 2023, https://snl.no/dialekter_i_Noreg; Ernst Håkon Jahr, *Den store dialektboka* (Oslo: Novus, 1990).
37. Johannessen and Salmons, *Germanic Heritage Languages in North America.*
38. Johannessen and Salmons.
39. Johannessen and Laake, “On Two Myths of the Norwegian Language in America.”
40. Johannessen and Laake, 319.
41. Johannessen and Laake, 312.
42. Johannessen and Laake, 312.
43. Hjelde, “Changes in a Norwegian Dialect in America,” 283–84.
44. Haugen, *Norwegian Language in America,* 345.
45. Hjelde, “Changes in a Norwegian Dialect in America,” 294.
46. Janne Bondi Johannessen, “Attrition in an American Norwegian Heritage Language Speaker,” in Johannessen and Salmons, *Germanic Heritage Languages in North America,* 46–71.
47. Roman Jakobson, *Child Language, Aphasia, and Phonological Universals* (The Hague, Netherlands: Mouton Publishers, 1941).
48. Johannessen, “Attrition in an American Norwegian Heritage Language Speaker.”
49. Johannessen, 46.
50. Johannessen, 68.
51. Björn Lundquist, Maud Westendorp, and Bror-Magnus S. Strand, “Code-Switching Alone Cannot Explain Intraspeaker Syntactic Variability: Evidence from a Spoken Elicitation Experiment,” *Nordic Journal of Linguistics* 43, no. 3 (2020): 249–87.
52. Lundquist, Westendorp, and Strand, “Code-Switching Alone Cannot Explain Intraspeaker Syntactic Variability,” 265.
53. Lundquist, Westendorp, and Strand, 282.

REVIEWS

Carrie Hertz, editor. *Dressing with Purpose: Belonging and Resistance in Scandinavia.*
Bloomington: Indiana University Press, 2021. xvii + 238 pages.

Carol Colburn and Mae Colburn

This engaging and well-illustrated publication, which coincided with an exhibition at the Museum of International Folk Art (MOIFA) of the same title, offers a renewed theoretical formulation of Swedish *folkdrakt,* Norwegian *bunad,* and Sámi *gákti* and, by extension, of broader concepts such as fashion, costume, and traditional dress. By examining traditional dress within these three abutting, overlapping, and interconnected contexts, we learn about its role within familial relationships, nationhood and nation building, colonialism and assimilation, resistance to colonization, and Indigenous activism, as well as emigrant and immigrant expressions of distinction and belonging. These investigations support this volume's critical main point, which is that the meanings of traditional dress are multiple and ever-changing.

This volume moves from an introduction by editor Carrie Hertz, which offers a theoretical foundation, to three society-specific sections that include introductory essays by Hertz followed by case studies by guest authors. Combined, these sections present a thorough, updated history of each tradition, as well as a broad range of contemporary perspectives reflecting individual use. The editor and authors describe welcoming encounters with interlocutors connected to each tradition, which adds an element of storytelling. This methodology does ample justice to the theoretical premise that the meaning of traditional dress is created "in the space between wearers and beholders" (18).

The order of these sections, moving from Swedish, to Norwegian, to Sámi societies, reflects the content presented. In Sweden, we learn that what is left of the use of traditional clothing hearkens back to eighteenth- and nineteenth-century use. The Norwegian use of the bunad flourished in the twentieth century as a symbol of Norway's independence from Sweden and continues today as an evolving symbol of belonging and integration when, for example, worn with hijabs. In Sápmi, which spans parts of northern Norway, Sweden, Finland, and Russia, traditional dress was subject to colonizing forces for much of the twentieth century. It experienced a resurgence in the context of the Indigenous rights movement and continues to be revitalized through knowledge recovery and renewed interpretations.

Each section has its unique character, reflecting the historiography of each tradition. The Swedish section focuses on dress as collected and studied in museum settings, and a case study focuses on how a private family collection of folkdrakt has adopted museum methods for collection care. The section on Norway cites descriptive and analytical works from the twentieth century, updating them with case studies related to the bunad as worn in contemporary multi-ethnic Norway and diaspora communities in the United States. The section on Sámi gákti incorporates descriptions of current revitalization over a long period of forced assimilation. This section concludes with a poetic chapter describing the reintroduction of *ládjogahpir,* a headdress forbidden by Christian religious authorities, into communal knowledge streams.

Describing all three traditions within a single volume is innovative and reflects the volume's origin in an American museum setting. Most research into Scandinavian traditional dress overlooks the potential for comparison demonstrated in this volume. The stories told here unfold in relation to each other, and the reader benefits from the variety of content and scholarly approaches. This volume also turns an informed lens onto museums themselves, reflecting on MOIFA's history of exhibitions related to Scandinavian and Sámi traditional arts. In the conclusion, Hertz comments on the tendency of museums in general to "sort the world and its people into conceptually bounded and named objects for comparison" and describes her attendant responsibility to understand the power of "naming" and place this process back in the field, which this volume does so well (216).

We recommend this volume to a global audience of makers, wearers, and owners of traditional dress, fashion and design historians, and scholars of colonial and Indigenous histories. In the United States, this updated understanding will inform contemporary exchanges between U.S. and Scandinavian wearers of traditional dress described in the essay written by Laurann Gilbertson. This volume reinforces the value, complexity, and intentionality inherent in custom clothing that is intended to be worn for decades and passed down through generations.

Carol Colburn *is professor emerita from the University of Northern Iowa. She holds a PhD in textiles and clothing within the College of Human Ecology at the University of Minnesota.*

Mae Colburn *holds a master's in the history of design and curatorial studies from Parsons School of Design.*

Olaf Minge, Kyle Ward, and Erik Brun, editors. *The Viking Battalion: Norwegian American Ski Troopers in World War II.* Havertown, PA: Casement Publishers, 2023. xxxvii + 378 pages.

Christopher Sterba

In this work, twenty-eight veterans, nearly all of Norwegian descent, describe their experiences serving in one of the most extraordinary combat units of the Second World War. Trained to fight as ski troopers, the soldiers' original purpose was to spearhead an offensive that would liberate Norway from Nazi occupation. Instead, the Ninety-Ninth Infantry Battalion (Separate) landed on the beaches of Normandy soon after D-Day. Traveling on the backs of tanks rather than on skis, they saw heavy action in France, Belgium, Holland, and Germany. When the war in Europe ended, their work was not over, as they were next assigned to their country of origin, helping the Norwegian population recover from five years of Nazi rule. *The Viking Battalion,* edited by Olaf Minge, Kyle Ward, and Erik Brun, not only offers a moving narrative of the men's service but also highlights the long-overlooked responses of America's Norwegian diaspora to the Second World War.

The editors have organized the soldiers' accounts carefully, beginning with brief historical overviews written by unit members at different times since 1945. This first third of the book establishes a timeline and framework for understanding the personal memories of the men, who frequently stress, in the many chapters that follow, how little they knew about the larger context of the war they were fighting.

Their story begins in the fall of 1942, when the War Department created a 1,000-member unit composed exclusively of "men who can read and speak Norwegian" (361). Early in the war, the army activated a number of ethnic units, made up of immigrants or persons descended from Norway, Greece, Austria, and the Philippines, populations that had been occupied by the Axis powers. The men who volunteered for the Ninety-Ninth came from all across the country and included many Norwegian nationals who had escaped the German invasion in 1940. Assembling in Minnesota, they were sent to Camp Hale in the

Colorado Rockies, where they endured the army's toughest training regimen of the war. The members vividly recall the fifty-mile hikes they completed on skis and snowshoes in subzero conditions. Yet the Ninety-Ninth's unique character and purpose kept them highly motivated. As Lt. Robert T. Bjorgum writes, since "everybody was of Norwegian extraction or from Norway . . . we had a feeling of oneness, I think. I don't think there was anyone in the military that was as close as we were. Even amongst the officers and enlisted men, we were a close-knit unit" (263).

By the time the ski troopers sailed for Europe, however, their mission had completely changed. Landing in France in late June 1944, they found themselves attached in quick succession to a variety of airborne, armored, and infantry units. The "99ers" helped to win victories in Belgium's canal district and the city of Aachen, Germany, and fought in frontline positions during the Battle of the Bulge for thirty-one straight days. The men tell of surviving bombing and strafing attacks and constant artillery shelling, of battling tanks while engaged in house-to-house fighting, and seeing friends killed suddenly by sniper fire. When sharing these memories, they often confess an inability to describe the violence and destruction they witnessed. And while at times nostalgic for the camaraderie and pride they felt, many are candid about the friendly fire they encountered and are openly critical of the Allies' unnecessary bombing of civilian homes and factories.

Their responsibilities away from the front lines, meanwhile, are as diverse and compelling. A small contingent of the Ninety-Ninth helped to treat the survivors of Buchenwald and bore witness to the concentration camp's horrors. Others guarded the vast quantities of gold and looted art the Nazis had hidden in mines toward the end of the war. It was the unit's last assignment in Oslo that was the most unifying of the men's experiences. For several months after VE Day, the battalion helped to oversee the removal of the 300,000 German soldiers still in Norway. The process went smoothly, allowing the members ample time to visit relatives and old homesteads and participate in major public events, most notably the return of King Haakon VII and the Norwegian government-in-exile and the soldiers' own celebration of the Fourth of July.

It is at moments like these, when the veterans' sense of a transcultural ethnic identity comes to the foreground, that one wishes the book could have included more of their thoughts, feelings, and backgrounds. Perhaps this could be the subject of a smaller companion volume by the Ninety-Ninth Infantry Battalion Educational Foundation, the group founded to preserve this important history. But even without that focus, this work is a very welcome contribution to the field.

Christopher Sterba *teaches in the American Studies program at San Francisco State University. He was the Fulbright Professor of American Literature and Culture at the Universitetet i Bergen in 2012–2013. Sterba is the author of* Good Americans: Italian and Jewish Immigrants during the First World War *(Oxford University Press).*

Elisabeth Koren. *Brev hjem 1853–1858*. Edited by Øyvind Tveitereid Gulliksen.
Oslo: Det norske språk—og litteraturselskap/bokselskap.no, 2021. 373 pages.
https://www.bokselskap.no/boker/korenbrevhjem/tittelside

Elisabeth Koren. *Brev hjem 1859–1867*. Edited by Øyvind Tveitereid Gulliksen.
Oslo: Det norske språk—og litteraturselskap/bokselskap.no, 2023. 450 pages.
https://www.bokselskap.no/boker/korenbrevhjem2/tittelside

Kari G. Hempel

Elisabeth Koren's letters home, *Brev hjem 1853–1858* and *Brev hjem 1859–1867,* are now published for the first time. Koren is already known for her diary *The Diary of Elisabeth Koren 1853–1855* (1955). Recently, a remarkable collection of her letters home has been found. It is the largest collection of migrant letters written by a single Norwegian emigrant, a total of 146 letters. The letters provide new insight about Norwegian immigrants in the Midwest in the mid-nineteenth century and new information about the Norwegian-American church in its early phase. The content, as well as the external circumstances, make the collection unique.

Professor Emeritus Øyvind Tveitereid Gulliksen was asked by Luther College to work on the letters. He has interpreted, systematized, and transcribed the letters and supplemented the text with extra information to facilitate greater understanding. In addition, volume 1, *Brev hjem 1853–1858,* contains a rich preface that places the texts within a historical context and the literary genre of America letters. The new information greatly increases the meaning and use of the texts.

Who was Elisabeth Koren b. Hysing (1832–1918)? She was from the town of Larvik, Norway. Her father, Ahlert Hysing, was the headmaster of the local preparatory Latin school and a respected mayor for eight years. He represented Larvik and Sandefjord in Stortinget (the National Assembly). Their family resided in Herregården (the manor) in Larvik, a magnificent building from the seventeenth century with an unusually large garden. The garden is often mentioned in the letters. The Hysing family was well-off, and Elisabeth's greetings home to families such as Treschow (landowner), Archer (the Colin Archer family), and Cappelen (the county governor) testify to her family's social position in the city.

At the age of twenty-one, Elisabeth married her second cousin, Vilhelm Koren (1826–1910). After his theological examination in 1853, Vilhelm received a call from Norwegian settlements in northern Iowa, USA, for a priestly position. He accepted the position. In August of the same year, he and Elisabeth got married, and in September they left Norway. Vilhelm Koren was to become one of the leading pastors within the Norwegian Synod, which considered itself a representative of the Norwegian State Church in the United States.

Elisabeth started writing during the journey to the United States, a diary as well as letters. Writing was to become her "most important passion," as she predicted in a letter at the turn of the year 1853/1854. Her background often appears in her writings. In the United States, Elisabeth encountered a culture she barely knew from the homeland, a Norwegian farming culture. It offered surprises such as a new degree of social equality: "*You,* they all say now, both to me and to Vilhelm" (25 December 1853).[1] Elisabeth was surprised that she did understand most Norwegians: "I didn't think it would be as easy to talk to them as it is. It is also easy for me to understand most people. I didn't expect that" (25 December 1853). In another letter, she teases the family at home: "Aren't you afraid that we will become quite peasant-like (-)?" (13 September 1855). Elisabeth eventually appreciated the qualities of the society she encountered.

In the first period, the Koren couple had a simple life. For some months, they shared a small cabin with another couple. In the sleeping area only a curtain separated the couples' beds. Later, they borrowed a small house, before they took over the parsonage, not yet finished before they moved in. However, the letters contain little of complaining, either about hard work or material conditions. During the period of time Elisabeth wrote the letters, she gave birth to seven children. She seemed to handle the practical challenges with the growing family very well. She was proud of the healthy children who at the time (in 1867) were the only grandchildren in the Helsing family.

Elisabeth read news about Europe in the newspapers, especially in *Emigranten,* a Norwegian-American publication. She worried about the situation in Europe, first the Crimean War and later the German–Danish War, and she was upset that the Danes were left alone against the superior German force. The American Civil War also raged in the United States during the period. She writes about it, but it receives surprisingly little attention. During the Civil War, a Native American rebellion took place in Minnesota—the US–Dakota War. The rebellion is mentioned, but little is written about the violence or the outcome. Elisabeth is concerned with reassuring her family back home that there is no danger where they live.

The immigrant church was the first major joint initiative among the Norwegian Americans. This commitment is reflected in the letters. Elisabeth writes a lot about her husband's ministry, the many parish trips, and Vilhelm's importance and efforts to establish Luther College. The college opened in Decorah in 1865.

The topic of slavery, a difficult issue in the Norwegian Synod, is discussed both directly and indirectly in the letters—indirectly through a description of pastor Claus L. Clausen. It is well known that Clausen left the Norwegian Synod because of the leadership's view on slavery. It is less known how this was perceived in the congregations. Clausen was initially a close friend of the Koren family. When he removed himself from the synod's theological line, their perception of Clausen changed. On 22 May 1854, Elisabeth wrote, "I was really fond of Clausen." On 12 June 1862, his change of mind is described as "to little credit." On 14 May 1865, he was not "one of the decent ones," and on 21 November 1866, he was "just as awkward." Clausen held a leading position in the three biggest Norwegian synods, successively. It is therefore interesting to see how he was perceived by Koren during this period of his career.

Who will be interested in these letters today? The collection ought to be of great interest to researchers and students who study Norwegian migration to the United States and living conditions among early immigrants. Furthermore, researchers who study Norwegian-American church history (e.g., the debate about slavery, the development of congregational and organizational history, and college history) have got a new valuable voice to listen to. The letters also represent a treasure trove for historians who study local history related to the Larvik municipality and Decorah, Iowa, and surroundings. For literary researchers, the writing style, the narratives, and the captivating travelogues might be of interest. The fact that the letters are easily accessible online makes an investigation easier for all interested readers.

Kari G. Hempel *is a retired associate professor in history at the University of Stavanger. She has done research on Norwegian-American congregations and studied the role of religion in various migration processes.*

NOTE

1. The translations of the quotes are my own and have been made informally.

Edvard Hoem. *Haymaker in Heaven*. Translated from the Norwegian [*Slåttekar i himmelen*, Forlaget Oktober] by Tara Chace. Minneapolis: Milkweed Editions, 2022. 324 pages.

Ingrid Urberg

Over the past decade, critically acclaimed Norwegian author Edvard Hoem has written seven novels about the extended family, descendants, and ancestors of Knut Hansen Nesje, a haymaker who leased a small parcel of land above the town of Molde, Norway, in the latter part of the nineteenth century. The first volume of this best-selling historical fiction series in Norway is now, fortunately, available to a much broader audience with this English-language edition, skillfully translated by Tara Chace.

The events in *Haymaker in Heaven* take place from 1874 to 1892, a time of great social, political, and economic change in Norway, and the novel traces the fortunes and movements of Nesje and his family members as they navigate life during this period of mass emigration and industrialization. While Nesje and the other characters are named after and inspired by Hoem's own family members, including his great-grandfather Nesje, Hoem makes it clear that his characters are fictitious. However, family stories, church records, newspaper articles, and other documents have informed how he has chosen to create these figures. Nesje, his wife, Serianna, and Serianna's sister Gjertine are strong and memorable characters, and Gjertine is particularly colorful, notable for her reading prowess, ability to stanch blood, outspokenness, and independence. She is not a stereotypical reluctant female immigrant. Indeed, in addition to being the first in her family to express the wish to move to America, a wish that is fulfilled when she convinces her husband Ole to immigrate to the Dakota Territory, she becomes the primary farmer in her family since Ole is taken up with his work as a saddler. While surveying the prairie during the move, she "was filled with a joy for which she had no words. It was like her prayer was answered" (193).

The reader quickly becomes invested in the journeys, joys, challenges, and disappointments of Hoem's characters, both those who remain in Norway and those who emigrate to what is now South Dakota, and the novel smoothly alternates between these settings. Hoem describes the ways in which the novel's numerous characters negotiate their relationships with spouses, parents, siblings, and children as major life decisions are made—marriage, child-rearing, choice of livelihood, etc.—in Norway and the Midwest. These choices are informed by social, economic, religious, and other circumstances, and Hoem does not overlook the impact of class and gender in these situations. While Nesje and Serianna stay in Norway, they have multiple family members who eventually move to Dakota, and the question of why some Norwegians chose to emigrate and others chose to stay in Norway is embodied in the lives of Hoem's characters.

It is clear that Hoem has carefully researched social, political, religious, and economic conditions in Norway and the Midwest at the end of the nineteenth century, and he deftly weaves references to historical movements, figures, and events into the narrative. These include suffrage in Norway and the United States, the power of America letters, typical travel routes and shipping lines used by Norwegian immigrants at this time, the works and influence of authors Henrik Ibsen and Bjørnstjerne Bjørnson, and the celebration of the Seventeenth of May (syttende mai). Information about midsummer traditions in Quebec, a point of transit for the immigrants, as well as the Children's Blizzard of 1888, the flora and fauna of the midwestern prairie, and fleeting interactions and trade with the Dakhóta people are also effectively integrated into the novel. Hoem comments on the role of Norwegians in colonization when he notes how Gjertine's brother Ola erected barbed wire fences, "and with that came the end of the time when Native people and white people could live side by side. . . . They had to stay on reservations and avoid the land that white people had taken" (269).

At times, additional comments have been added to the original text to provide framing for those who may be unfamiliar with the Norwegian cultural context—for example, the poet Ivar Aasen is mentioned by name in the English edition, a statement unnecessary in the Norwegian text where he is only referred to as "the poet." Only a few of these adjustments were necessary, however, since the original does a fine job of contextualizing terms such as *Readers* (followers of the lay preacher Hans Nielsen Hauge) for today's audience. This brings us to the translation of Hoem's Nynorsk text itself.

Tara Chace's translation does justice to Hoem's distinctive, poetic style, and a fine example of this is her rendering of Hoem's multipage description of the art of haymaking and working with a scythe. "Of all the pilgrimage paths our Lord prepared, the one that runs through hay is most beautiful" (239). It is important to note that Hoem (b. 1949) writes in Nynorsk, one of the two official written norms of Norwegian. In addition to being a novelist and dramatist, Hoem is also a poet and translator, and as such is keenly interested in maintaining the stylistic integrity of the original text. The Hoem–Chace partnership is successful in this regard.

One has to wait until the very end of the novel to appreciate the book's title, and readers will likely be left with a desire to read how Hoem's vividly painted and memorable characters continue to fare on both sides of the Atlantic. When this work is placed in the context of the seven-volume series, one can draw comparisons between Norwegian Ole E. Rölvaag and Swedish Vilhelm Moberg's multivolume works about migration, and hopefully English translations of the other rich volumes in Hoem's series will become available in the near future.

Ingrid Urberg *is professor of Scandinavian studies at the University of Alberta Augustana Campus. Her research interests include personal narratives and polar literature, and she is currently working on an oral history project titled "The Norwegian Immigrant Experience in Alberta."*

Gunnar Nerheim. ***Norsemen Deep in the Heart of Texas: Norwegian Immigrants, 1845–1900.***
College Station: Texas A&M University Press, 2024. 392 pages.

John Weinstock

Gunnar Nerheim has written a fine book about Norwegian immigration to Texas in the latter half of the nineteenth century. The title of the book might bring back memories of the 1941 hit song with lyrics by June Hershey and music by Don Swander. In this case though, it refers to a county in the state of Texas—Bosque County (*bosque* is Spanish for "woods")—that became the home of many Norwegian immigrants. When did Norwegians begin coming to North America? In 1825 the sloop *Restauration* carried fifty-two Norwegian Quakers/Haugeans, including Cleng Peerson, over the Atlantic to New York City. Over the ensuing years, Cleng Peerson would play an important role in the settlement of Norwegians in the United States. Nerheim's book is a compendium of all imaginable information about how Norwegians got to Texas in the nineteenth century, why they decided to leave their native land, where in Norway they came from, what made them undertake such a hazardous journey, how they managed to cross the Atlantic Ocean, where they arrived in North America, their destinations on the new continent, why Bosque County—and much more. Connections/choices might be the most appropriate metaphor for this book's focus. A Norwegian decides to go to the New World for an opportunity to lead a better life. Where does she come from? How would she reach the New World? In the nineteenth century this meant traveling by boat. Sailboat or steamship? The former would take much longer—up to three months. Where would the boat land? What would the new arrival's destination be? How would she get from the port to where she wanted to go? Did she have any ideas about where she was headed? Perhaps she had gotten a letter from someone (a relative, perhaps) who had already made the journey. What role would illness and disease play? In short, there were myriad scenarios.

The book consists of an introduction, fourteen chapters, and four appendixes, plus notes, bibliography, and index. There is a wonderful gallery of photos in the middle. The chapter titles are informative. Here are three examples: "Johan Reinert Reiersen and the First Norwegian Migration Chain to Texas"; "Cleng Peerson, the Father of Norwegian Immigration, Goes to Texas"; "Why Did Immigrants from Hedmark County in Eastern Norway End Up in East Texas?" Keep in mind that Texas is a big state; its area is roughly 80 percent more than all of Norway. For example, Bosque County is situated in the north-central part of Texas, northwest of Waco. In the nineteenth century, this meant that Norwegian emigrees were not far from Native Americans. Nerheim relates the story of fourteen-year-old Ole Tergerson Nystøl, who was captured by Comanche but managed to survive for three months and then escaped. Others were captive for years. One of many reasons Norwegians ended up in Bosque County was health. In counties further to the east there were problems with "climate fever" and ague, which eventually led to many of those Norwegians moving west to Bosque County.

The number of Norwegians that came to Texas was relatively small compared to those who found their way to the Upper Midwest. Nerheim provides figures for Norwegian immigrants in the United States in 1860. For example, there were 21,442 in Wisconsin, 8,428 in Minnesota, 5,668 in Iowa, and 4,891 in Illinois, yet only 326 in Texas (4). Cleng Peerson (1783–1865), from Tysvær in the county of Rogaland, Norway, was the pathfinder, the most important figure in the emigration of Norwegians to North America and their subsequent settlement. He had led a group of settlers to a spot on the Illinois River near the Fox River Valley. After 1838, he returned to Norway at least twice and then settled in Lee County in southeastern Iowa. In 1842, he joined a group of Swedish immigrants at Bishop Hill in Illinois. In 1854, the Texas legislature granted him 320 acres west of Clifton in Bosque County.

Nerheim lists the personal wealth of twenty-six Bosque County residents in 1860 (from $10,145 to $54,091) and the number of enslaved people owned by fifty-one enslavers, as well as the enslavers' places of birth (appendixes 2 and 3). In 1860, there were 105 Norwegians in Bosque County (appendix 1). None of them are represented in either of the two lists. In 1860, there were 516 Norwegians in Texas, of whom 306 were Norwegian-born. Nerheim's book contains many more gems that should be of interest not only to those with Norwegian roots but to others in Texas and beyond. Today, if someone with Norwegian roots wished to learn more about their own family history, this book would likely be very useful to them.

John Weinstock *earned his PhD at the University of Wisconsin and taught at the University of Texas from 1966 to 2011, focusing on Norwegian language and Sámi culture. He has published many articles and reviews and several books, including a cotranslation with Turid Sverre of Alfred Hauge's* The True Saga of Cleng Peerson *in 1983.*

Erik Aalvik Evensen. *Rabulisten: Johan Reinert Reiersen (1810–1864).* Tvedestrand, Norway: Bokhuset Forlag, 2022. 369 pages.

Øyvind T. Gulliksen

In an essay published in 1962, Einar Haugen argues that a book-length study ought to be written about Johan Reinert Reiersen, a person whom Haugen then considered to be a significant member of what he calls "a kind of fraternity of founding fathers" in the history of Norwegian emigration to America.[1] Erik Aalvik Evensen has published a book-length biography of Reiersen entitled *Rabulisten: Johan Reinert Reiersen (1810–1864).* It may not be the in-depth study that Haugen had in mind, but it is an intriguing study of Reiersen's entire life from his childhood in Holt, a small community in Southern Norway, to his death in Texas in 1864.

Reiersen is best known as the leader of Norwegian emigration to Texas during the 1840s. In 1844, after a visit to the United States and Texas, he published a very popular book entitled *Veiviser for norske emigranter til de forenede Nordamerikanske Stater og Texas.* According to historian Odd S. Lovoll, this book and others of the kind served as "extended America letters . . . eagerly read by people who intended to emigrate."[2]

Reiersen's upbringing in Norway is a major point in Evensen's book. He points out that during the mid-1800s, his home community of Holt became a strong local center in education as well as finance. Farms were improved, local industry flourished, and higher education became possible to gifted young people. In fact, Holt is now often referred to as a kind of precursor to the University of Agder in Kristiansand.[3]

Johan Reiersen was the first of nine children born to Kirsten and Ole Reiersen in Holt. Ole was a teacher and served as a sexton in the local church, not an unusual combination at the time. With financial support from Jacob Aall, a prosperous owner of a local ironworks, Johan Reiersen and a few others received financial support to study in Christiania. But, as both Haugen and Evensen point out, things went wrong for Johan at the university, basically caused by a controversy between him and his cousin, Knud Knudsen, also from Holt, who later became a central language reformer in Norway. In 1838, at the age of twenty-eight, Johan settled in Kristiansand, where he started his own newspaper, *Christiansandsposten,* in which he supported liberal ideas. He also invited the poet Henrik Wergeland (1808–1845) to contribute to the newspaper.

On the issue of emigration, Reiersen openly disagreed with Wergeland. Reiersen saw emigration to America as a logical consequence of liberal ideas of the time. Wergeland, however, urged Norwegians to stay home. In 1843 and 1844, Reierson traveled extensively in the United States and Texas. His recommendations were enough to attract a large group of emigrants from Landvik (near Grimstad) to Texas, but to them Texas was not the success that Reiersen had dreamed of (203–10). Evensen shows why this group had every reason to doubt Reiersen's optimism (203).[4]

Evensen ends his book with a long section on Elise Wærenskjold (1815–1895) and her lifelong friendship with Johan Reiersen. It was almost certainly Reierson who made her emigrate to Texas in 1847. In his conclusion, Evensen could have meditated on Elisabeth and Johan's well-known letter from Texas to Norway, written in February and May in 1848, and sent to Taale A. Gjestvang.[5] This letter proves that the two letter writers represented a Norwegian-American renewal of a liberal culture they had both encountered in the Norwegian village in which they had grown up. Johan argues that what to him in Texas appears as "the naked Truth" [*den soleklare Sandhed*] in Norway is referred to as "Lies and Deceit."[6] In the same letter, Elise argues that rich people may well stay in Norway but "the poor [*de Fattige*] would be far better off if they could come here."[7]

In 1962, Einar Haugen argued that Reierson's first trip to Texas should not be seen "as a second flight from failure," comparable to his first failure in the capital of Norway.[8] In a sense, Evensen's book proves Haugen right. For Johan and Elise, Texas was a place to go. Both Johan Reiersen and Elise Wærenskjold argued for a Texas-based Norwegian-American liberalism.

Øyvind T. Gulliksen *earned his PhD at the University of Bergen. A professor emeritus of American studies at the University of South-Eastern Norway, he is the author of* Twofold Identities: Norwegian-American Contributions to Midwestern Literature *(2004) and numerous articles on Scandinavian-American literature. He has an honorary degree from Luther College.*

NOTES

1. Einar Haugen, "J. R. Reiersen's 'Indiscretions,'" *Norwegian-American Studies* 21 (1962): 270.
2. Odd S. Lovoll, *The Promise of America: A History of the Norwegian-American People* (Oslo: n.p., 1984), 14.
3. See Ernst Håkon Jahr, *Nybrottsmannen Andreas Faye* (Oslo: Novus forlag, 2021).
4. See Anna Igland Bendixen et al., *Vandring ut. Emigrasjon fra Landvik, 1840–1960* (Grimstad, Norway: Landvik Historielag, 2012).
5. Orm Øverland and Steinar Kjærheim, *Fra Amerika til Norge. Norske utvandrerbrev 1838–1857,* vol. 1 (Oslo: Solum forlag, 1992), 113–18.
6. Øverland and Kjærheim, *Fra Amerika til Norge,* 114.
7. Øverland and Kjærheim, 118.
8. Haugen, "J. R. Reiersen's 'Indiscretions,'" 275.

NOTES FROM THE FIELD

Crossings

THE BICENTENNIAL OF NORWEGIAN MIGRATION TO NORTH AMERICA

Amy L. Boxrud

As I write this in early 2024, anticipation is building for next year when Crossings, the bicentennial of organized Norwegian migration to North America, will be commemorated on both sides of the Atlantic. The bicentennial marks the voyage of the sloop *Restauration,* sometimes called the "Norwegian Mayflower," from Stavanger to New York in 1825.

In North America, what began as a prepandemic conversation around a table at the Vesterheim Museum has grown into an online planning group representing more than thirty organizations across the continent. We envision a series of events leading up to and spread throughout 2025, held throughout Norway, Canada, and the United States. Our aim is to create an umbrella organization that supports partner organizations in commemorating the bicentennial in ways that are fitting to their own missions. Vesterheim and NAHA, both founded as part of the legacy of the 1925 Norse American Centennial a century earlier, have shared responsibility for calling the meetings. An executive committee to further facilitate planning began meeting in 2023. The *Norwegian American* newspaper hosts and maintains our website, and Norway House serves as fiscal agent.

CROSSINGS
NORWAY & NORTH AMERICA
1825 · 2025

Figure 1. A transatlantic committee developed the Crossings logo with Replace Design of Minneapolis. The logo is available to partner organizations in English, Norwegian, Sámi, and French.

From the start, we did not envision a bicentennial that would closely resemble the 1925 Norse American Centennial. Held in the wake of WWI nativism and the

Figure 2. Norse American Centennial draft logo, 1925. Courtesy of the Norwegian American Historical Association in Northfield, Minnesota.

Immigration Act of 1924, the centennial is remembered for its contrasting goals of cultural preservation and assimilation and was viewed by some in the Norwegian immigrant community as an opportunity to enhance their status in American society. A century later, the players may have changed, but anti-immigrant attitudes are still prevalent. We hope that Crossings can be a positive voice in this conversation, with participants more fully appreciating the complexities of migration for individuals, families, nations, and Indigenous peoples.

A rewarding aspect of this planning has been the collaboration between Norwegian and North American organizations. A subcommittee with members from Norway and North America worked together to develop the common Crossings identity. In keeping with the original voyage of the *Restauration,* a replica of the sloop is scheduled to leave Norway on July 4 and arrive in America on October 9. Events and exhibits on both sides of the Atlantic will frame and provide context for the voyage. NAHA will cohost a conference exploring the causes and impact of Norwegian migration, together with Det norsk-amerikanske historielaget i Norge (NAHA-Norge), the Norwegian Researchers and Teachers Association of North America (NORTANA), and the Norwegian Department at St. Olaf College. With events geared for both scholars and the public, the gathering is scheduled for June 18–22 on the St. Olaf campus. By the time this article is published, information on many more events will be available. To learn more and to find a Crossings event near you, visit crossings.norwegianamerican.com.

***Amy L. Boxrud** has served as executive director of the Norwegian American Historical Association since 2015. Her interests include public history and Nordic folk arts.*